D1116774

Diseases and Disorders

Parkinson's Disease

Diseases and Disorders

Parkinson's Disease

Titles in the Diseases and Disorders series include:

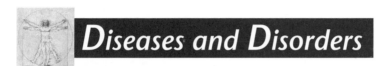

Diseases and Disorders

Parkinson's Disease

by Melissa Abramovitz

LUCENT
BOOKS®

THOMSON
™
GALE

San Diego • Detroit • New York • San Francisco • Cleveland
New Haven, Conn. • Waterville, Maine • London • Munich

On cover: Doctors view deep brain stimulation surgery being performed on a Parkinson's disease patient to help relieve some symptoms of the disease.

LIBRARY OF CONGRESS CATALOGING-IN-PUBLICATION DATA

Abramovitz, Melissa, 1954–
    Parkinson's disease / by Melissa Abramovitz.
       p. cm. — (Diseases and disorders)
    Includes bibliographical references and index.
Summary: Discusses the origins and causes of Parkinson's disease, as well as treatment and research. Ways of coping and living with the disease are also discussed.
    ISBN 1-59018-300-2 (hard cover : alk. paper)
    1. Parkinson's disease—Juvenile literature. I. Title. II. Series: Diseases and disorders series.
    RC382.A274 2004
    616.8'33—dc22
                                                                    2004010198

Printed in the United States of America

Table of Contents

"The Most Difficult Puzzles Ever Devised"

CHARLES BEST, ONE of the pioneers in the search for a cure for diabetes, once explained what it is about medical research that intrigued him so. "It's not just the gratification of knowing one is helping people," he confided, "although that probably is a more heroic and selfless motivation. Those feelings may enter in, but truly, what I find best is the feeling of going toe to toe with nature, of trying to solve the most difficult puzzles ever devised. The answers are there somewhere, those keys that will solve the puzzle and make the patient well. But how will those keys be found?"

Since the dawn of civilization, nothing has so puzzled people—and often frightened them, as well—as the onset of illness in a body or mind that had seemed healthy before. A seizure, the inability of a heart to pump, the sudden deterioration of muscle tone in a small child—being unable to reverse such conditions or even to understand why they occur was unspeakably frustrating to healers. Even before there were names for such conditions, even before they were understood at all, each was a reminder of how complex the human body was, and how vulnerable.

While our grappling with understanding diseases has been frustrating at times, it has also provided some of humankind's most heroic accomplishments. Alexander Fleming's accidental discovery in 1928 of a mold that could be turned into penicillin

8

has resulted in the saving of untold millions of lives. The isolation of the enzyme insulin has reversed what was once a death sentence for anyone with diabetes. There have been great strides in combating conditions for which there is not yet a cure, too. Medicines can help AIDS patients live longer, diagnostic tools such as mammography and ultrasounds can help doctors find tumors while they are treatable, and laser surgery techniques have made the most intricate, minute operations routine.

This "toe-to-toe" competition with diseases and disorders is even more remarkable when seen in a historical continuum. An astonishing amount of progress has been made in a very short time. Just 200 years ago, the existence of germs as a cause of some diseases was unknown. In fact, it was less than 150 years ago that a British surgeon named Joseph Lister had difficulty persuading his fellow doctors that washing their hands before delivering a baby might increase the chances of a healthy delivery (especially if they had just attended to a diseased patient)!

Each book in Lucent's Diseases and Disorders series explores a disease or disorder and the knowledge that has been accumulated (or discarded) by doctors through the years. Each book also examines the tools used for pinpointing a diagnosis, as well as the various means that are used to treat or cure a disease. Finally, new ideas are presented—techniques or medicines that may be on the horizon.

Frustration and disappointment are still part of medicine, for not every disease or condition can be cured or prevented. But the limitations of knowledge are being pushed outward constantly; the "most difficult puzzles ever devised" are finding challengers every day.

An Ancient Disease

MEDICAL HISTORIANS SAY that what is now known as Parkinson's disease has existed since ancient times. The first documented reference was in the Sanskrit texts of ayurvedic medicine practiced in India. Written around 2500 B.C., these texts described different patterns of tremor in a so-called shaking palsy. A similar disorder was mentioned in the first Chinese medical textbook, *Nei Jing*, published twenty-five hundred years ago. An Egyptian papyrus written between 1350 and 1200 B.C. also described a king with symptoms of stiffness and tremor that sound a lot like what are today known as symptoms of Parkinson's disease.

During the Middle Ages the physician Galen described a similar disorder that included tremor, paralysis, and a shuffling gait. In the early 1500s artist and inventor Leonardo da Vinci, who also studied anatomy and physiology, talked about a disease in which "nerves sometimes operate by themselves without any command from other functioning parts or the soul. This is clearly apparent for you will see paralytics and those who are shivering and benumbed by cold move their trembling parts, such as their heads or hands without permission of the soul; which soul with all its forces cannot prevent these parts from trembling."[1] Other experts subsequently wrote about this disease that was referred to as the "shaking palsy" or "paralysis agitans," the Latin term, but it was not until 1817 that James Parkinson, for whom the disease was named, wrote the first formal description.

Parkinson was born in London, England, on April 11, 1755. He became a physician and began practicing medicine in 1785. Not only was he a skilled and dedicated doctor, but he was also a social activist and published pamphlets and books on the social ills of the times as well as on geology and paleontology. He also wrote books on a variety of medical topics. In 1817 when he published "An Essay on the Shaking Palsy," the first formal description of Parkinson's disease, it received little recognition. Later on, however, realizing the essay's value and the clarity of Parkinson's observations, doctors named the disease after him.

The essay described the major symptoms and stages of the disease based on Parkinson's observations of six patients. It spoke

Renaissance artist Leonardo da Vinci, who made this and other detailed sketches of the human anatomy, was one of the first people to document the symptoms of Parkinson's disease.

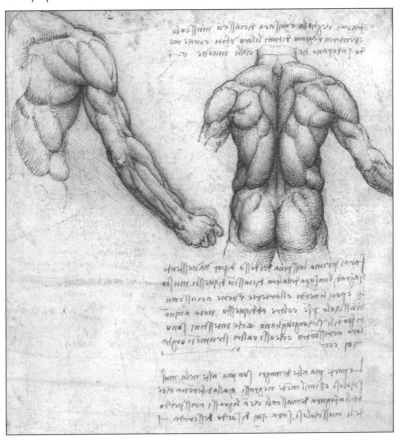

of "involuntary tremulous motion, with lessened muscular power, in parts not in action and even when supported; with a propensity to bend the trunk forwards, and to pass from a walking to a running pace: the senses and intellect being uninjured."[2] Modern doctors say his observations were extremely perceptive for the era in which he lived. He did err in not recognizing that the disease could affect the senses and intellect as well as motor skills, but his writings were otherwise so complete that modern physicians still read his original notes and essay since they remain relevant to modern medicine.

Even though Parkinson's description of the disease was mostly accurate, he did not correctly determine what caused the disorder and he had no idea of how to treat it. He hypothesized that it was caused either by drinking liquor or by sleeping on the bare earth, as a sailor who developed the disease did for several months in prison. Both suppositions were inaccurate. In fact, no one achieved a real understanding of the processes involved until the mid-twentieth century. At that time doctors gained insight into the underlying brain changes behind the disease and discovered the first effective treatment for the disorder.

But even with this treatment and with other new therapies, the disease continues to make life extremely difficult for those it affects. Today, researchers are working all the time to develop newer and better treatments. Thanks to the efforts of several celebrities with the disease, such as actor Michael J. Fox, boxer Muhammad Ali, former U.S. attorney general Janet Reno, and the late U.S. congressman Morris Udall, along with many lesser-known activists, funding for research has increased significantly over the past several years. Patients with Parkinson's disease today have reason to be optimistic as this research makes the possibility of a cure more and more realistic in the foreseeable future.

Chapter 1

What Is Parkinson's Disease?

PARKINSON'S DISEASE IS a disorder of the central nervous system, that is, of the brain and spinal cord. Since it primarily involves problems with movement, Parkinson's disease belongs to a group of conditions known as motor system disorders. Sometimes the disease is referred to as the "shaking palsy," as Parkinson originally described it, and sometimes it is called "paralysis agitans," the Latin term.

The disease is chronic, meaning that it persists over time and does not go away once someone has it. It is also progressive, meaning that its symptoms worsen over time. According to the authors of *Parkinson's Disease: A Complete Guide for Patients and Families,* "Because Parkinson's disease is a progressive disorder, we can generally expect that each year the signs and symptoms of the disease will become more pronounced. No one, not a physician or anyone else, can accurately predict how, or how quickly, the disease will progress in a specific individual."[3]

In most cases, the disease progresses slowly over many years, but this can vary among individuals. No matter how quickly or slowly it progresses, the disease itself does not significantly decrease a person's life expectancy. People do not usually die from Parkinson's disease, though they may succumb to some of the problems brought on by the disease such as falling or inhaling food into the lungs, which can lead to pneumonia.

Primary Symptoms

Parkinson's patients typically exhibit some or all of a variety of symptoms. The severity varies from patient to patient and tends to grow worse over time.

One of the primary symptoms is rigidity. This looks like a stiffness in the muscles. It increases during movement and is responsible for the masklike expression on the faces of many people with Parkinson's. In some patients, rigidity results in pain, particularly in the arms and shoulders. It also tends to cause pain and spasms in the feet.

There are two types of rigidity associated with Parkinson's disease. One is known as lead-pipe rigidity. This is a smooth resistance that a doctor can feel when examining the person's muscles. The second is called cogwheel rigidity. Here, stiffness in the muscles causes muscle movement to look like a cogwheel in motion.

Another primary symptom of the disorder is tremor or shaking, the symptom most often identified with Parkinson's disease. Not all patients, however, experience tremors.

For those who do experience this symptom, tremors may involve the arms, legs, hands, head, neck, and face. Often a tremor is the first symptom that people notice. The tremors often begin on one side of the body, frequently in one hand. Then they progress to other areas on that same side of the body. Later on, tremors may spread to the other side of the body.

Tremors are most severe when the person is at rest and are reduced when the person is moving. The degree or intensity of tremors may also vary throughout the day and may worsen with any sort of emotional excitement. Tremors generally disappear during deep sleep.

Another primary symptom is slowness of movement, also known as bradykinesia. This results from a delay in the brain's instructions to certain parts of the body and also from a slow response to carrying out those instructions. According to the National Institute of Neurological Disorders and Stroke, "Bradykinesia, or the slowing down and loss of spontaneous and automatic movement, is particularly frustrating because it is unpredictable. One moment the patient can move easily. The next moment he or she may need help. This may well be the most disabling and distressing symptom of the disease because the patient cannot rapidly perform routine movements."[4]

Poor balance is another symptom that affects many people with Parkinson's disease, especially when they move suddenly. This can result in repeated falls and injuries. Often patients develop a forward or backward lean or a stooped posture while standing that further exacerbates balance problems.

Walking or gait problems are also common. These may include a decrease in arm swings, causing the arms to hang rigidly by the

Legendary boxer Muhammad Ali suffers from Parkinson's disease. His primary symptoms include muscle rigidity in his shoulders and a masklike facial appearance.

sides, as well as short, shuffling steps, difficulty turning, and sudden "freezing" spells during which the person cannot take the next step. Other times, a patient may suddenly shift from a walking gait to a running gait.

Secondary Symptoms

A variety of other symptoms are known as secondary since they arise from the primary symptoms of Parkinson's disease. One serious secondary symptom that affects as many as 50 percent of Parkinson's patients is depression. People who are depressed lose

Many Parkinson's patients experience severe depression as a secondary symptom. Changes in the brain caused by the disease often exacerbate their depressed condition.

The lack of muscle control Parkinson's disease patients experience can cause them to choke while trying to swallow.

interest in life, feel sad and useless, and do not want to socialize much or cope with new situations. Experts say some of the depression results from the brain changes that lead to Parkinson's disease, whereas some involves a patient's response to the disability brought on by other symptoms. Many people with Parkinson's also become very anxious about many things, and this can worsen their depression.

Speech problems are also a very common symptom. Many patients speak so slowly and softly that others cannot hear or understand them. They may also hesitate before each word or slur their words. Problems with certain muscles and muscle control also frequently lead to swallowing difficulties. This can cause the person to cough or choke while eating or drinking. It may also allow saliva to pool in the mouth with subsequent drooling. The tongue may not drop down to let food pass into the throat from the mouth, which can lead to difficulty getting food or liquids into the throat. The throat muscles may also be affected and may not pass food completely into the esophagus. This can result in food entering the airways, causing choking. The food can even get into the lungs and cause pneumonia. This occurs because the food inflames the lungs and induces the production of mucous that can clog the airways.

Muscles in the chest wall and diaphragm may also become rigid and nonfunctional in Parkinson's disease, leading to breathing problems. Shortness of breath is common because the lungs do not expand fully when the person inhales, nor do they relax fully when the person exhales. This results in the person breathing at a higher-than-normal rate and becoming short of breath.

Other common symptoms of Parkinson's disease include small, cramped handwriting and sleep disturbances such as trouble staying asleep at night, restlessness, nightmares, and daytime drowsiness. Oily skin on the face and scalp, excessive sweating, constipation, and sexual difficulties are other frequently seen symptoms. Dementia, in which the person has trouble thinking and remembering things, and weight loss are other common problems. Even those who continue to consume their usual number of calories tend to lose weight. Experts believe this may be because tremors and rigidity require more calories than the person usually burns or because the disease itself promotes metabolic defects that lead to weight loss.

Similar Disorders and Parkinson's Disease

Not all patients with Parkinson's disease have all of these symptoms, and many of the symptoms also occur in other diseases. This can make diagnosis difficult. Some of the other diseases easily confused with Parkinson's are progressive supranuclear palsy, multiple system atrophy, diffuse Lewy body disease, and Alzheimer's disease. These diseases share many symptoms with Parkinson's disease, but they have different causes and treatments, so it is important that a correct diagnosis be made.

Progressive supranuclear palsy is a rare brain disorder that causes problems with gait and balance. Patients cannot direct their eyes properly because of lesions, or sores, in the brain areas that control eye movements. They also frequently show depression and dementia.

Multiple system atrophy is a degenerative disease of the nervous system characterized by symptoms affecting movement, blood pressure, and other body functions. These symptoms include stiffness, slowed movements, loss of balance, and incoordination. Male impotence, urinary difficulties, constipation, speech and swallowing difficulties, and blurred vision are also typical.

Diffuse Lewy body disease primarily affects thinking and intellectual functioning, but may also include Parkinson's-like movement symptoms. Lewy bodies are abnormal structures that grow in certain nerve cells in the brain, leading to a variety of problems. Diffuse Lewy body disease affects different parts of the brain than Parkinson's disease, so the disease process is very different.

Alzheimer's disease is a disorder in which a loss of brain cells leads to a decline in memory and thinking skills. Disorientation,

An elderly woman suffers from Alzheimer's disease, the symptoms of which are sometimes mistaken for Parkinson's.

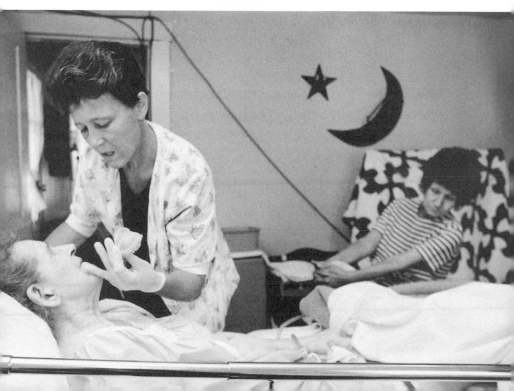

anxiety and agitation, and an inability to perform daily tasks are also common, so sometimes this disease is mistaken for Parkinson's disease.

Parkinsonism

Besides these diseases that may be confused with Parkinson's disease, other movement disorders share symptoms of Parkinson's disease but are not true instances of the illness. Parkinsonism is the name given to a group of disorders that share symptoms such as rigidity and tremor but result from different processes than those that underlie true Parkinson's disease. Examples include arteriosclerotic parkinsonism, in which damage to blood vessels from several small strokes leads to Parkinson's-like symptoms, and drug-induced parkinsonism, a reversible disease in which certain drugs produce these symptoms. In drug-induced parkinsonism, the symptoms disappear when the drugs are discontinued. True Parkinson's disease, in contrast, is not yet reversible since it results from damage to specific brain cells.

Because these similar disorders may appear much like true Parkinson's disease, sometimes a correct diagnosis takes several years; a physician must often watch as symptoms progress to see which disease is really present. This can be frustrating for both the patient and the doctor, but is sometimes unavoidable because of the similarities. "Accurate diagnosis of neurologic movement disorders is tricky, even in the best of hands. As many as one in five persons with Parkinson's receives a misdiagnosis,"[5] say the authors of *Parkinson's Disease: A Complete Guide for Patients and Families.*

Knowledge about cases of misdiagnosis comes from long-term follow-up studies and confirmation of the diagnosis during an autopsy. An autopsy can reveal the underlying brain changes responsible for a particular disease.

Experts say, however, that the chances of a misdiagnosis are reduced by going to an experienced physician. Parkinson's authorities recommend that people consult a neurologist who specializes in motor disorders to obtain the most accurate assessment. Many such specialists belong to the Movement Disorders Society, a professional organization for doctors who specialize in Parkin-

or not a patient is suffering from Parkinson's disease. One such test is a motor physiology test. It involves measuring the force and speed with which the person performs certain tasks such as reaching for targets or copying spirals.

Neuroimaging

Recent technology has provided another type of diagnostic test called neuroimaging that allows a physician to measure directly the nerve cells in a specific area of the brain affected by Parkinson's disease. This area is called the substantia nigra, and the nerve cells involved are called dopamine neurons. These cells secrete the chemical messenger, or neurotransmitter, dopamine. Parkinson's disease destroys these cells.

One neuroimaging technique is a Positron Emission Tomography (PET) scan. Here, a doctor injects the patient intravenously with a chemical that causes dopamine neurons to light up when viewed with a scanner. This scanning machine can gauge whether there are an abnormally low number of dopamine neurons in the substantia nigra. If so, this means that the patient probably has Parkinson's disease. The PET test can also be used to assess how fast or far the disorder progresses over time.

The PET scan uses very low levels of radioactivity, and experts say it poses very few risks to patients. It is not used very often, though, because it is so expensive, costing twenty-five hundred to six thousand dollars. Many medical insurers will not cover this expense.

Usually, however, says Dr. Steven Frucht in an article written for the Parkinson's Disease Foundation newsletter, this test is not necessary. He explains, "In the vast majority of cases, the UPDRS and the neurologic examination are more than sensitive enough to make the diagnosis. . . . The key factor in diagnosing Parkinson's is not the complexity or sophistication of the technology, but the skill and specialization of the doctor."[6] Some doctors disagree with this opinion, stating that neuroimaging is a much more accurate method of diagnosis, but the fact remains that these tests are still not frequently used because of the expense.

After the Diagnosis

Whatever the means employed, having diagnosed Parkinson's disease, a doctor will then determine which of several stages the patient is in. Sometimes these stages are numbered, but most experts simply refer to the stages as early, moderate, and advanced.

In the early stages, symptoms may be subtle and not interfere much with daily life. In many cases, the symptoms appear gradually before the obvious symptoms such as tremor become evident. Patients with very early symptoms may be tired or slightly shaky. They may have difficulty getting out of a chair. They may begin to speak softly or lose track of thoughts or words. Family members may notice that the person's face lacks expression or that the individual moves more slowly than normal. The person may report feeling internal tremors that cannot yet be seen.

Soon, in the moderate stages, symptoms usually become more pronounced. Rigidity and tremors begin to interfere with daily life. Swallowing may become difficult. Sleeplessness, pain, and depression may be evident. By the time they get to this stage, most people have sought medical help to determine what is wrong.

In the advanced stages, symptoms worsen, even when treated with medication. Movement becomes extremely slow. Pain becomes more pronounced. Communication is significantly impaired in the advanced stages. Other people may have great difficulty understanding the patient's speech. Handwriting may become illegible. Swallowing may become increasingly difficult, making it a chore for the person to eat, drink, and swallow medication. Mental functioning may deteriorate; about one in four people with Parkinson's develops dementia severe enough to interfere with daily functioning.

No one can predict how rapidly these stages will progress or how disabled an individual will become, as this varies widely from person to person. Some patients do not get much worse for five, ten, or more years, whereas others deteriorate rapidly over a short period.

Who Gets Parkinson's Disease?

No one can predict who will get Parkinson's disease. Virtually anyone can. It is found in all parts of the world and affects all races and socioeconomic classes. In the United States, experts estimate that about 1.5 million people are affected. Men get Parkinson's more often than women, but plenty of women get the disease too. The disease is most common in older people, but younger ones also get it. The average age of onset is sixty, but the disorder can and does strike younger people. The general public is much more aware of this since the actor Michael J. Fox developed the disease at age thirty and became an advocate for research to defeat it.

Actor Michael J. Fox attends a Parkinson's benefit with his wife. After developing the disease, Fox established a foundation to support Parkinson's research.

Experts report that 4 to 12 percent of Parkinson's patients in the United States and Europe develop the disease before age forty. In Japan, up to 40 percent of Parkinson's patients develop it before age forty. This high rate of young-onset Parkinson's in Japan is probably due to genetic factors.

Doctors refer to cases of Parkinson's disease that develop in patients between the ages of twenty-one and forty as young-onset Parkinson's disease (YOPD). They refer to patients who develop the disease before age twenty-one as having juvenile parkinsonism (JP). JP is not characterized as true Parkinson's disease because the brains of people with JP do not display some of the same defects as those of patients with true Parkinson's disease. The symptoms also tend to vary. Patients with JP usually show turning in of both feet early on in the disease, and they rarely have tremors. The major symptoms of JP are rigidity, slowness of movement, and cramps and painful spasms of the feet.

Patients with YOPD and JP tend to show symmetrical symptoms. This means that both sides of the body are affected equally. If one hand is rigid, the other one is too. This is different than in adult-onset Parkinson's disease, where symptoms tend to start on one side of the body. The disease also progresses more slowly in YOPD and JP patients than in adult-onset Parkinson's. In YOPD mental changes such as dementia are rarely present either.

Many cases of YOPD and JP go undiagnosed, at least for a while, because doctors do not expect Parkinson's disease or parkinsonism in young people. Richard, for example, had many symptoms of Parkinson's but, as he explains, was not diagnosed initially:

> When I was 24 years old, my symptoms were apparent, but because of my age and general overall good health, I went undiagnosed. I had the symptoms associated with a typical Parkinson's patient: slowness and loss of movement, postural instability resulting in frequent falls, a distorted gait and muscle rigidity. I remember not going on a family vacation because my body ached so badly and I was so stiff and rigid that walking consumed all my energy. Because of a common misconception that Parkinson's disease is a geriatric disorder, the diagnosis wasn't as obvious as it should have been.[7]

The consequences of a failure to diagnose Parkinson's correctly means that such patients go through potentially harmful therapies or receive no treatment at all. Some are told the problem is all in their head and are diagnosed as mentally ill. They waste time in psychiatric care or even endure surgery that will not help them. Patients who are misdiagnosed also suffer emotionally because they know something is wrong and are frustrated not knowing what the problem really is.

Eventually, as symptoms become more apparent and the correct specialists are consulted, most people in this predicament will receive a proper diagnosis and can then begin to address the many issues that accompany having Parkinson's disease.

Chapter 2

What Causes Parkinson's Disease?

PARKINSON'S DISEASE IS caused by a loss of certain cells in the central nervous system. The central nervous system is made up of neurons and glial cells in the brain and spinal cord. Neurons are nerve cells. They transmit information using electrical impulses and chemical messengers. Glial cells support neurons.

Neurons comprise three basic parts. One is the cell body, which contains a nucleus that controls the cell's activities and contains the cell's genetic information. The other parts are axons and dendrites. Axons look like long tails. They transmit messages from the cell. Dendrites look like tree branches. They receive messages for the cell. Neurons communicate through these axons and dendrites by sending chemicals called neurotransmitters across a tiny space known as a synapse.

There are three major classes of neurons. Sensory neurons carry information from the sense organs, such as the eyes and ears, to the brain. Motor neurons have long axons and carry information from the central nervous system to the muscles and glands throughout the body. Interneurons communicate only in their individual area and have short axons. Within these three major classes of neurons are hundreds of subtypes, each able to perform specific message-carrying functions and to produce different neurotransmitters.

Disruptions in the transmission of neural communications can occur at any point in the chain of neurons. The areas of the brain that are affected to produce symptoms of Parkinson's disease are primarily the substantia nigra and the basal ganglia. These areas in turn influence motor neurons that carry commands throughout the body.

The substantia nigra is a small area located deep within the brain. The name means black substance, and it was so named because cells in this area are dark. This region of the brain is filled with neurons that produce the neurotransmitter dopamine. These neurons deliver dopamine to other parts of the brain, including the basal ganglia, which are part of the pathway that helps control motor signals from the brain. The basal ganglia are located at the

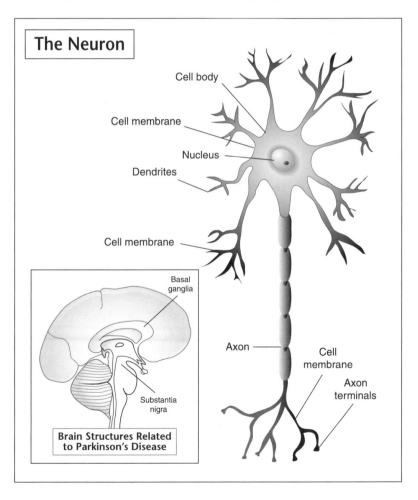

The Neuron

Cell body

Cell membrane

Nucleus

Dendrites

Cell membrane

Basal ganglia

Axon

Cell membrane

Axon terminals

Substantia nigra

Brain Structures Related to Parkinson's Disease

base of the brain. The parts of the basal ganglia important in Parkinson's disease are the globus pallidus and the striatum.

Dopamine normally sends signals that allow a person or animal to move smoothly and normally. In Parkinson's disease, however, dopamine-producing cells in the substantia nigra are damaged or destroyed. The dopamine supply to the striatum in particular is severely disrupted. This in turn leads to disruptions in the motor signals coming from the striatum, leaving an individual unable to direct or control motion in a normal manner. Muscles may tighten up at inappropriate times, producing tremors and rigidity. Movement is slowed by the inadequate communication between the brain and the muscles. The autonomic nervous system, the part of the nervous system that automatically controls body temperature, digestion, bladder control, and sexual function, may also be affected by this process, leading to other characteristic symptoms of the disease.

Parkinson's disease damages the brain cells that produce dopamine, a neurotransmitter that regulates movement. Here, a researcher uses a computer model to study dopamine receptors in the brain.

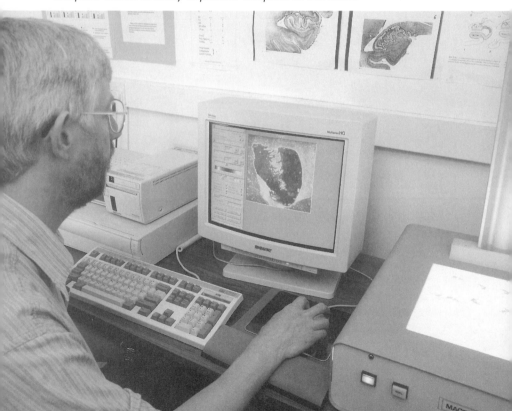

Studies show that people with Parkinson's disease may lose 80 percent or more of the dopamine-producing cells in the substantia nigra. In fact, the symptoms of the disease usually do not become apparent until about 80 percent of these cells have died. This is because the nervous system has many redundancies and safety factors that take over the actions of the dying cells. Only when a large number of cells have died are these safety factors no longer able to compensate for their loss of function.

When the brains of Parkinson's disease patients are viewed at autopsy, the substantia nigra has lost its usual black pigment due to the loss of its neurons. The cells that do remain in this area are abnormal; that is, they display small bodies known as Lewy bodies that researchers believe play a role in the death of these neurons.

Other Neurotransmitters Involved

Besides dopamine, other neurotransmitters are also involved in Parkinson's disease. Damage to dopamine-producing cells has been shown to upset the balance between dopamine and the neurotransmitter acetylcholine, which is also important in movement. This imbalance can further exacerbate the symptoms of Parkinson's.

The neurotransmitters norepinephrine and serotonin are also affected in Parkinson's disease. Norepinephrine regulates blood pressure, pulse rate, perspiration, and other stress-related responses; and these functions may be affected in Parkinson's disease. Serotonin is involved in mental and emotional functioning, and disruptions in its balance can lead to depression, anxiety, and other emotional disorders. These problems are often seen in Parkinson's patients.

Gamma-aminobutyric acid (GABA) and glutamate are other neurotransmitters that scientists believe play a role in Parkinson's disease. GABA is an inhibitory chemical, whereas glutamate is excitatory. That is, one inhibits neurons, and the other excites them. When the balance of these chemicals is disrupted, some of the sleep disorders and movement problems associated with Parkinson's

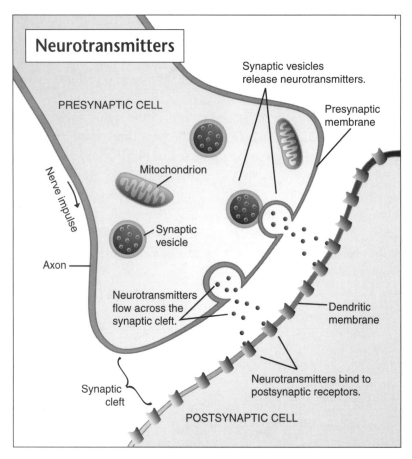

disease can result. The lack of dopamine found in Parkinson's disease also contributes to problems created by an imbalance of GABA and glutamate. Dopamine normally helps to balance the effects of glutamate, and when it is not present, the globus pallidus area in particular may be overstimulated.

Underlying Causes

While the deficiency of dopamine neurons is known to cause Parkinson's disease directly, the factors that cause the initial destruction of dopamine neurons are not quite as clear-cut. Scientists are conducting a great deal of research to determine exactly what these factors are, and so far it appears that both genetic and environmental influences are involved. "Scientists generally agree that Parkinson's disease is likely to be 'multi-factorial'—that is, it has a variety of causes,"[8] according to the Parkinson's Disease Foundation.

One underlying cause currently the subject of much research is genetics. Genes are the part of a deoxyribonucleic acid (DNA) molecule that transmits hereditary information from parents to offspring. They reside on wormlike bodies called chromosomes in the center, or nucleus, of each cell. The sequence of genes on each chromosome provides the cell containing those chromosomes with a set of instructions on how to grow and operate. A baby is born with two copies of this instruction set—one from each parent.

Humans have forty-six chromosomes in each cell, with the exception of mature sex cells, which have only twenty-three. Twenty-three of the forty-six chromosomes come from the mother and the other twenty-three from the father. The genes on each chromosome also come in pairs, with one copy of every gene from the mother and one from the father.

When a gene or chromosome is damaged, the resulting change is called a mutation. Mutated genetic material can be passed to a child if it happens to be part of the set of chromosomes and genes transmitted from either the mother or father. When this occurs, the altered genetic instructions may cause various malfunctions that produce certain diseases or disorders.

Genetics and Parkinson's Disease

Scientists have shown that some instances of Parkinson's disease are linked to gene mutations, whereas others are not caused by a particular gene mutation but instead are linked to a genetic predisposition toward the disease. A predisposition means that some people inherit a tendency to develop the disease if certain environmental factors are also present. Recent scientific studies indicate that several genes may be involved in such a genetic predisposition. One is the gene that regulates the tau protein. The tau protein is important in allowing the flow of nutrients through nerve cells. According to one of the authors of a study at Duke University Medical Center reported in November 2003, "Tau is the first example of a gene thought to be involved in susceptibility leading to late-onset Parkinson's disease. Tau by itself does not cause Parkinson's, but we found that a form of the protein may make some people susceptible to Parkinson's disease."[9]

Other genes that scientists suspect are involved in causing a susceptibility to Parkinson's disease promote the metabolism of iron. Researchers have found iron deposits in the brains of Parkinson's patients, and animal research suggests that genetic defects that impair iron metabolism may play a role in causing the disease. Further research is planned to gather more data on these genes in the hope that someday knowledge of the mechanisms involved will lead to methods of preventing or treating Parkinson's disease.

In contrast to genes that govern a tendency toward Parkinson's, there are also specific gene mutations that directly cause the disease in some cases. This usually occurs in young-onset Parkinson's disease, but not always. One group of such genes have been labeled

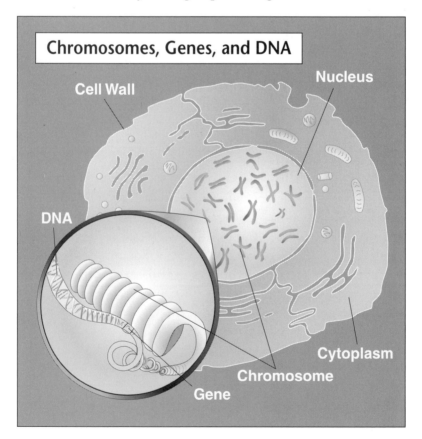

Chromosomes, Genes, and DNA

Cell Wall

Nucleus

DNA

Cytoplasm

Chromosome

Gene

PARK 1, 2, 3, 4, 5, 6, 7, 8, and 10. PARK 1 was the first Parkinson's-related gene to be discovered back in 1997. Scientists discovered mutations in this gene in large Italian and German families that had many cases of early-onset Parkinson's disease. PARK 1 is responsible for the function of the protein alpha-synuclein. Mutations in the PARK 1 gene can cause abnormal clumping of this protein. The abnormal clumps, called Lewy bodies, are linked to the dopamine neuron destruction that underlies Parkinson's disease.

PARK 6 is another recently discovered gene related to Parkinson's disease. Researchers found it by examining the DNA of people in an Italian family with many members having Parkinson's disease that started between the ages of thirty-two and forty-eight. Most of the symptoms in these people occurred on one side of the body, and the disease progressed slowly in all of them. The researchers concluded that mutations in the PARK 6 gene were most probably responsible for the particular characteristics of the disease in this family and in others with similar symptoms.

The parkin gene is another gene linked to the development of Parkinson's disease. Parkin mutations were first linked to cases of early-onset Parkinson's in 1998, but subsequent research also found mutations in the gene in some people with late-onset Parkinson's. It appears that people with early-onset Parkinson's related to this gene inherit two defective copies of the parkin gene, one from each parent, whereas those with late-onset cases inherit only one defective copy. Researchers believe that this may explain why some people with mutations in this gene develop the disease earlier than others.

Another gene that appears to influence the onset of Parkinson's disease is known as ST01 (glutathioneS-transferase, omega-1). ST01 seems to be associated with a late onset in both Parkinson's disease and Alzheimer's disease. The gene is linked to inflammation in the brain, and further knowledge of it can also lead to an understanding of whether inflammation is involved in the development of Parkinson's and Alzheimer's diseases.

Environmental Influences

In addition to genetic influences that trigger the destruction of dopamine neurons that underlies Parkinson's disease, several environmental factors also appear to play a role.

There is strong evidence that certain chemicals such as pesticides and herbicides cause Parkinson's disease. One study found that exposure to these chemicals caused a 50 to 70 percent increase in the risk of Parkinson's. Other studies indicate a high incidence of Parkinson's among people who are agricultural workers or who drink private well water that can become contaminated with these substances. A 2001 study showed that the combination of two widely used pesticides creates a pattern of brain damage in mice exactly like that seen in human Parkinson's patients. These substances are the herbicide paraquat and the fungicide maneb. Both are used extensively in the United States on many crops. The researchers who conducted the 2001 study believe that many other harmful combinations of chemicals are also used every day, exposing people and animals to extensive neurological damage. Says the lead researcher at the University of Rochester School of Medicine in Rochester, New York, "In the real world, we're exposed to mixtures of chemicals every day. There are thousands upon thousands of combinations. I think what we have found is the tip of the iceberg. . . . This is the first time that truly environmental risk factors for Parkinson's disease have been identified."[10]

Other research has shown that the pesticide rotenone can cause the abnormal Lewy bodies that lead to Parkinson's disease. Rotenone, made from several plants, is used to kill insects in gardens and on farmland. It is also used to kill fish in reservoirs and lakes. Researchers at Emory University in Atlanta, Georgia, showed that injecting rotenone into laboratory rats caused major symptoms of Parkinson's disease and led to degeneration of dopamine neurons. The researchers point out that people and animals would not receive such massive exposure to the chemical in a natural environment, but that long-term exposure to rotenone may indeed build up and lead to Parkinson's disease.

Industrial chemicals and metals such as manganese, copper, lead, iron, mercury, zinc, and aluminum are also strongly linked to Parkinson's disease. In fact, in one study, researchers found that people who consume high levels of iron and manganese in their diet have a much increased risk of developing Parkinson's disease. This risk may actually lead to the development of the disease in

A crop duster sprays pesticides over an orchard. Research has demonstrated a compelling link between chemicals such as herbicides and pesticides and Parkinson's disease.

those who also have a genetic predisposition. The scientists believe this may be because in large quantities these chemicals are poisonous to nerve cells and may build up in the brain, causing the destruction of dopamine neurons in the substantia nigra.

Another chemical known as MPTP (1-methyl-4-phenyl-1,2,3, 6-tetrahydropyridine) is also strongly linked to Parkinson's disease. This link was discovered in the 1980s when a group of heroin addicts in California who had taken drugs contaminated with MPTP developed severe and sudden Parkinson's disease. Scientists later used the knowledge that this chemical causes the disease to give MPTP to laboratory animals so they would develop Parkinson's. This advanced research into the disease because now researchers could easily create laboratory animals with Parkinson's and then study them.

Other Environmental Influences

Besides these chemicals, other environmental influences are linked to the development of Parkinson's. One factor that has caused some controversy among experts is head trauma. Some studies have found that people who experience head trauma have a much greater risk of later developing Parkinson's disease, whereas other researchers find no correlation between head trauma and the disorder. One widely cited study found that people with severe head traumas that resulted in loss of consciousness, skull fractures, or bruising on the brain were especially likely to develop Parkinson's about ten years later. The doctors who conducted this study believe that the trauma may have disrupted the function of some neurons and thus may have later contributed to the development of the disease. This has not yet been proven, but some experts believe

Some studies have concluded that severe head trauma, such as that caused by the blows that boxers sustain, can lead to the onset of Parkinson's.

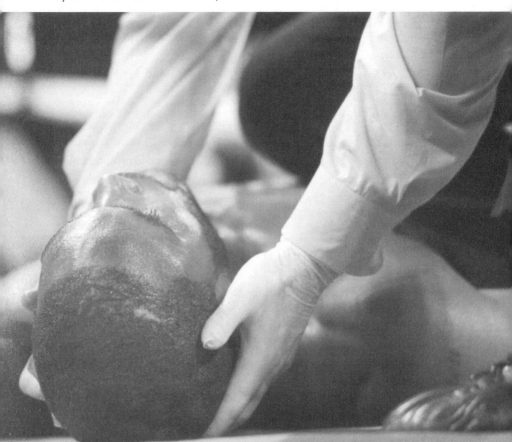

that such a process may be one contributing environmental factor. Others believe that head trauma can cause parkinsonism. This type of disorder seems to affect many boxers who receive repeated blows to the head. The rationale for labeling such damage as parkinsonism rather than as true Parkinson's disease is that the symptoms do not result from destruction of dopamine neurons but from other sorts of brain damage. The controversy over whether head trauma actually causes Parkinson's disease or parkinsonism is ongoing at this point.

Other environmental factors that may influence whether or not someone develops Parkinson's disease are combining caffeine, the drug in coffee, with female hormones. Some studies show that drinking coffee protects men, but not women, from getting Parkinson's. Researchers believe this may be because caffeine loses its protective ability when combined with female hormones. Other research indicates that caffeine itself may not protect people at all from Parkinson's. A large study that looked at more than seven thousand people found that those who drank coffee, smoked cigarettes, or drank alcohol had a lower-than-normal risk of developing Parkinson's disease. The investigators in this study believe that this is not because caffeine, tobacco, or alcohol themselves offer protection from the disease. They believe that people who engage in these so-called novelty-seeking behaviors have higher natural levels of dopamine in the brain. These higher levels of dopamine, rather than the caffeine, alcohol, or tobacco, are what may protect people from the disease.

Other drugs besides caffeine, alcohol, and tobacco have been linked to Parkinson's disease, but not in a protective fashion. These other drugs cause Parkinson's-like symptoms because they interfere with the brain's metabolism of dopamine. However, when these drugs are discontinued, the symptoms disappear, so they do not trigger instances of true Parkinson's disease. Drugs that can cause drug-induced parkinsonism include haloperidol and similar medications used to treat hallucinations and confusion, high blood pressure medications that contain reserpine, the antinausea drug metoclopramide, and some chemotherapy drugs used to treat cancer.

Underlying Chemical Changes

Whether the causes of Parkinson's disease originate in the environment, through genetic factors, or from some combinations of these forces, there appear to be several processes that occur at a cellular level that underlie the root cause of the disorder—the destruction of dopamine neurons. One is the formation of Lewy bodies, the abnormal clumps of the protein alpha-synuclein, in these nerve cells. Alpha-synuclein normally helps nerve cells communicate. However, this protein's abnormal clumping can keep the nerve cell from working properly, or it can kill it outright. Research shows that alpha-synuclein clumping can result from gene mutations or from environmental toxins. Either way, the result is the same.

Another cellular process that scientists believe contributes to Parkinson's disease is oxidative stress. Oxidative stress occurs when substances called free radicals interact with certain molecules. Free radicals are unstable molecules generated by chemical reactions in the body. They damage cells when they interact with molecules, including those of some metals such as iron. There is evidence that free radicals interacting with iron may contribute to the neuron destruction that accompanies Parkinson's disease. This evidence includes the finding that patients with Parkinson's have increased brain levels of iron and decreased levels of the chemical ferritin. Ferritin normally serves to protect brain cells from iron by forming a ring around the iron. In the absence of ferritin, the iron present can interact with free radicals, thereby damaging nerve cells.

The brains of people with Parkinson's disease also show reduced levels of glutathione, an antioxidant that helps to detoxify free radicals. Scientists believe that low levels of this chemical allow oxidation damage to occur, thereby leading to the destruction of dopamine neurons. Studies have shown that the lower the level of glutathione in the substantia nigra, the more severe the Parkinson's disease. This indicates that it is likely that this antioxidant plays a role in protecting the brain from the damage that causes Parkinson's.

Mitochondrial function is another cellular process that scientists believe plays a role in causing Parkinson's disease. Mitochondria are small energy-producing bodies within cells. Experiments with laboratory rats show that some environmental triggers for Parkinson's disease disrupt the mitochondria. For example, the pesticide rotenone causes a reduction in mitochondrial activity that is followed by Parkinson's symptoms. Rotenone and other pesticides increase the permeability of membranes surrounding the mitochondria, thereby allowing certain chemicals to leak out of them and destroy the cell.

Microglial cells also appear to play a role in causing Parkinson's. These cells nourish and support neurons in the brain. However, when certain chemicals or other influences stimulate microglial cells, inflammation may result; the microglial cells may also secrete toxic substances that kill neurons. Examination of the brains of deceased Parkinson's disease patients shows evidence of microglial cells that have been stimulated to produce toxic substances. Experts believe that these activated cells may cause some of the dopamine neuron destruction that underlies the disease. Further evidence that microglial cells may be involved comes from research with drugs that inhibit microglial activity. These medications seem to protect against dopamine neuron damage in the laboratory; investigators hope that someday such drugs can be used to help prevent or arrest Parkinson's disease in humans.

Other Cellular Influences

Trophic, or growth, factors are another cellular influence linked to the development of Parkinson's disease. These substances support neuron growth. They become reduced in the brains of older people, and experts believe this may contribute to the destruction of neurons that underlies Parkinson's. Researchers are experimenting with introducing trophic factors into the brain to try to prevent or reverse this cellular damage. One study showed that putting a trophic factor called glial-derived neurotrophic factor (GDNF) into the brains of monkeys with Parkinson's disease restored the production of dopamine and reversed symptoms of the disorder. The researchers hope this might work in humans as well.

The final cellular process that scientists are presently studying as a contributing factor to Parkinson's disease is abnormal apoptosis.

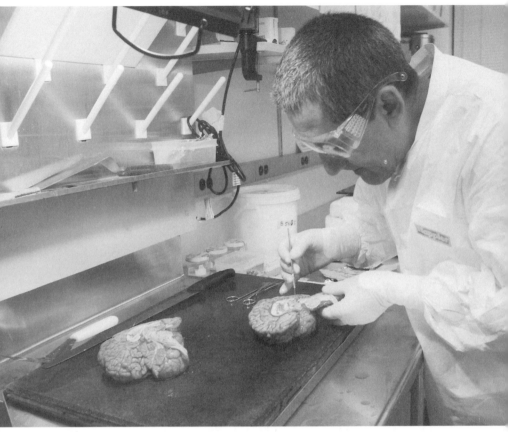

Examining the brains of deceased Parkinson's disease patients helps researchers better understand the neurological impact of the disease.

Apoptosis is the preprogrammed death of cells that normally occurs in the body. However, with Parkinson's disease, the process happens prematurely and at an abnormally high rate in dopamine cells. Researchers believe this may be due to a genetic defect that instructs the cells to die too soon. They are currently trying to find out exactly what goes wrong in this process so as to develop methods of stopping the premature cell death. One method of potentially interfering with premature apoptosis uses substances called caspase inhibitors. Caspases kill cells, so caspase inhibitors prevent cell death. In one study in Germany at the University of Tubingen, researchers were able to prevent the death of dopamine neurons by inserting genes for a caspase inhibitor and for a trophic factor into mouse brains. They hope that someday such a technique might prove viable for preventing dopamine cell death in humans, although this sort of interference can be dangerous since preventing cells from dying can lead to cancer.

Research on the cellular processes believed to underlie Parkinson's disease is bringing out a whole new variety of potential methods for the prevention and treatment of the disorder. This research is all very new, and for the first time, scientists are beginning to understand the full spectrum of underlying influences responsible for causing the disease.

Chapter 3

How Is Parkinson's Disease Treated?

T REATMENT OF PARKINSON'S disease is complex because of the wide range of symptoms and their severity, as well as the progressive nature of the disorder. This means that over time, a treatment plan must constantly be altered to meet the changing needs of the patient.

Treatment also involves several facets of care as the National Parkinson Foundation notes:

> Optimal care for persons with Parkinson's disease often includes a combination of pharmacologic and other interventions, such as physical, occupational, and speech therapy. Many patients also benefit from community social services and psychological counseling at points throughout their illness. The long-term goal of comprehensive therapy is to maximize current physical and mental function while maintaining options for a healthy future. [11]

Comprehensive treatment for Parkinson's disease is extremely expensive for patients and for society; many costs are paid by taxpayers when patients receive Medicare or disability payments. These total costs for all Parkinson's patients in the United States are estimated at $5.6 billion per year. Drugs to treat the disease run $1,000 to $6,000 per year per patient, and ongoing doctor visits can cost $5,000 per year or more. Hospitalization for Parkinson's-related falls alone runs $40,000 to $50,000 per patient on average, and those who require nursing home care may spend more than $100,000 each year.

Treatment with Drugs

The primary mode of treatment for Parkinson's disease is drugs. A variety of drugs are used to treat the disorder. Due to the wide range of symptoms and severity, the drugs and drug combinations used vary widely from individual to individual and over time in the same person. The precise drugs and combinations also depend on the patient's emotional reactions to various symptoms. For example, for some, tremors are not bothersome and therefore do not have to be treated. For others, tremors are disruptive or embarrassing, and the person insists on medication to relieve this symptom.

A Parkinson's patient with severe tremors tries to thread a needle. Many patients depend on medication to help control their tremors.

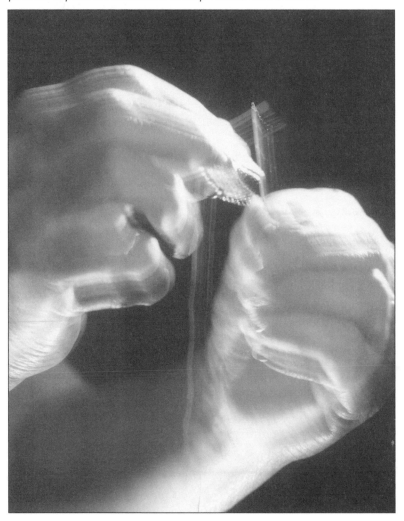

The degree to which certain symptoms affect an individual's activities also helps determine which drugs will be prescribed. Some people need longer-acting drugs to control symptoms day and night, whereas others are more concerned about controlling symptoms during the day. Once the drugs are started, different people have different reactions to them too. Some patients experience significant adverse effects from Parkinson's disease medications; others do not. Sometimes these effects are so serious that the medication must be discontinued.

It is challenging for a physician to prescribe exactly the right amount of medication so that symptoms that need treatment are addressed while significant adverse side effects are avoided. "It is unrealistic to expect medications to eliminate every trace of tremor, every trace of slow movement, every trace of gait impairment, or every trace of handwriting difficulty. To accomplish this with the current medicines, such high doses would be needed that the risks of serious side effects would greatly increase," [12] explain the authors of *Parkinson's Disease: A Complete Guide for Patients and Families.*

The Mainstay Drug to Treat Parkinson's

The primary drug used to treat Parkinson's disease is levodopa in varying forms and combinations. Levodopa is a form of dopamine discovered in 1957 by Dr. Arvid Carlsson of Sweden, who found that the substance could reverse the effects of Parkinson's disease in laboratory animals. Then, in 1960, the Austrian neuroscientists Herbert Ehringer and Oleh Hornykiewicz found that the brains of deceased human Parkinson's patients had a dopamine deficiency. Following this discovery, some doctors began giving levodopa to their patients, with no results until Dr. George Cotzias of Brookhaven Laboratories in New York found that giving very large doses of the drug could control symptoms. Before the discovery of levodopa, patients were sometimes given anticholinergic drugs to restore the balance of acetylcholine and dopamine in the brain. These drugs, however, were often not effective and had numerous side effects. They helped the resting tremor and drooling typical of Parkinson's, but did little else. Levodopa, on the other hand, does have side effects but also eases many of the symptoms of Parkinson's disease. It represented

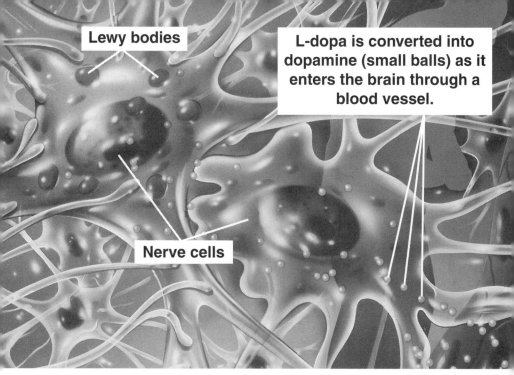

Lewy bodies

L-dopa is converted into dopamine (small balls) as it enters the brain through a blood vessel.

Nerve cells

An illustration shows nerve cells in the brain's basal ganglia being treated with the drug levodopa (L-dopa). Once it enters the brain, levodopa is converted into dopamine.

the first truly effective treatment for the disorder. "The drug revolutionized Parkinson's therapy, suddenly allowing people who had been wheelchair-bound and having extraordinary difficulty performing the activities of daily living to regain much of their ability to function normally,"[13] say the authors of *Parkinson's Disease: A Complete Guide for Patients and Families.*

Levodopa is a dopamine precursor—a substance that the brain transforms into dopamine. Dopamine itself cannot be used as an oral medication because it cannot pass through the blood-brain barrier. The blood-brain barrier is a biological mechanism in the body to keep poisons and other harmful substances out of the all-important central nervous system. The barrier allows only certain substances to pass through from the bloodstream to the brain. This mechanism works via a set of tightly packed cells in blood vessels entering the central nervous system.

Levodopa is one substance able to cross the blood-brain barrier. Once it enters the brain, the brain converts it to dopamine. This dopamine works just like naturally produced dopamine. Neuronal axons release it into the synapses between nerve cells; it attaches to receptors on dendrites on the next nerve cell, and so on. This process permits proper control of movement, temporarily relieving many symptoms of Parkinson's disease. Levodopa tends to work well for alleviating rigidity, tremor, bradykinesia, masklike facial expression, gait problems, and cramped handwriting. It is less effective in treating balance problems, speech problems, sexual dysfunction, excessive sweating, and pain. Numbness, oily skin, constipation, depression, and dementia are also not helped by levodopa.

A doctor writes a prescription for his patient. Although no cure for Parkinson's exists, doctors can prescribe drugs that alleviate many of the disease's worst symptoms.

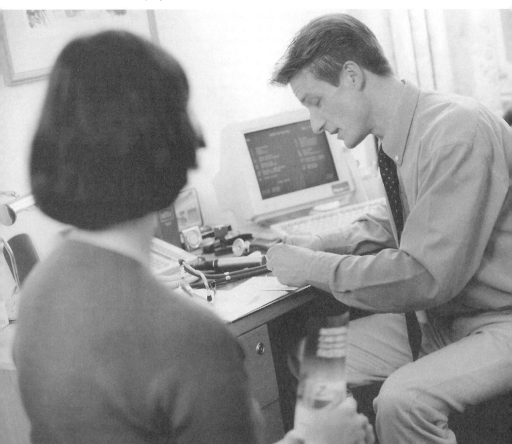

The effects of levodopa are only temporary, so the drug must be taken regularly to relieve symptoms adequately. The medication tends to wear off before the next dose, but taking it more frequently results in more severe side effects. These side effects include dyskinesias, which are involuntary writhing movements that involve the face, mouth, tongue, head, arms, trunk, or legs; severe nausea and vomiting; rapid heart rate; and lowered blood pressure upon standing up. Levodopa also becomes less effective over time, so physicians must often increase the dosage and dose frequency of the drug as the illness progresses, despite the side effects.

For a period after it was first introduced, doctors hoped that levodopa might be a cure for Parkinson's disease since it worked so well. However, the fact that levodopa becomes less effective over time shows that the disease continues to progress even when the drug is taken regularly.

Even though it is not a cure, levodopa combined with carbidopa is now the most prescribed drug for treating Parkinson's disease. This combination is marketed as Sinemet. It is an improvement over plain levodopa, since carbidopa prevents levodopa from being metabolized in the gastrointestinal system and in tissues in the rest of the body. This means more of the levodopa gets to the brain, so smaller doses are adequate. This cuts down on some of the adverse effects of the levodopa, especially on the nausea and vomiting, though many patients still experience these side effects depending on how large a dose of the drug they take and how frequently they take it.

In the early stages of Parkinson's, most patients take Sinemet two to three times daily. However, since it loses its effectiveness over time, later on in the disease more frequent doses are required. After Sinemet has been used for several years, many patients develop fluctuating responses to the drug. Doctors refer to these as "on" and "off" motor states. In the "on" state, the person responds well to the drug. In the "off" state, the person has more difficulties with movement. The "off" state often occurs just before the next medication dose is due, but it may also occur at random times. It is difficult for doctors to prescribe exactly the right dosage and frequency of administration to keep a patient in the "on" state as much as possible while also minimizing side effects. Another complication is that the drug must not be taken with meals, as proteins ingested may interfere with its absorption. Some people are advised to eat protein only at the evening meal if protein tends to interfere with Sinemet a great deal during the day.

There is now a timed-release formula known as Sinemet-CR that helps some patients with the "on-off" challenge. Sinemet-CR provides a slower release of the medication into the bloodstream and gives a longer duration of action.

Other Drugs

Since Sinemet does not alleviate all the symptoms of the disease, it is often used with other drugs to enhance its effects. Sometimes early on in the disease's progression some of these other drugs are used by themselves if Sinemet is not yet needed. All of the drugs used either by themselves or with Sinemet have potentially adverse side effects, but in most cases the benefits of taking them outweigh any unpleasant effects.

Anticholinergics, another drug group sometimes used, were the main treatment for Parkinson's prior to the introduction of levodopa. These include trihexyphenidyl, benztropine, mesylate, and procyclidine. By decreasing the activity of acetylcholine, these medications balance out the dopamine deficiency and tend to alleviate tremors and drooling in about 50 percent of the people who take them. Many doctors, however, are hesitant to prescribe anticholinergics because they can cause confusion and hallucinations; they are no longer used very often.

Dopamine agonists work by directly activating dopamine receptors in the brain. They are prescribed more frequently than are anticholinergics, either by themselves or in combination with Sinemet. Sometimes doctors prescribe them in the early stages of Parkinson's to delay the need for introducing Sinemet. Other times, dopamine agonists are combined with Sinemet to allow a dose reduction of the latter. When used in combination with Sinemet, dopamine agonists increase the amount of "on" time during which the patient gets relief of symptoms. Dopamine agonists include bromocriptine (mar-

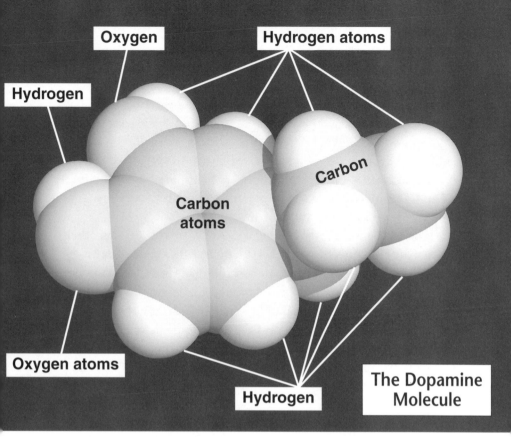

Oxygen

Hydrogen atoms

Hydrogen

Carbon

Carbon
atoms

Oxygen atoms

Hydrogen

**The Dopamine
Molecule**

A computer model of the dopamine molecule. Several drugs are available to Parkinson's patients that help stimulate the brain's supply of this vital neurotransmitter.

keted as Parlodel), pergolide (Permax), pramipexole (Mirapex), and andropinirole (Requip).

Symmetrel, also known as amantadine hydrochloride, is another drug frequently prescribed for Parkinson's patients. The drug increases the supply of dopamine in the synapses between neurons in the brain. It achieves this by either blocking the reuptake of dopamine by these neurons or by increasing the release of dopamine. It also inhibits the neurotransmitter acetylcholine. Symmetrel seems to be helpful in reducing the severity of dyskinesia and gait problems in many patients.

Doctors often prescribe Symmetrel by itself early on in the disease when symptoms are not too severe. Later on, when symptoms worsen, it may be necessary to add Sinemet to control these symptoms. Sometimes stopping Symmetrel for a while and then restarting it is also effective.

Selegiline, or deprenyl, is a monoamine oxidase B inhibitor that is often prescribed in the early stages of Parkinson's disease to delay the need for Sinemet. Monoamine oxidase B inhibitors work by inhibiting the enzyme monoamine oxidase B (MAOB) in the brain. MAOB interferes with the metabolism of dopamine, so inhibiting MAOB enhances the action of dopamine. In later stages, Selegiline seems to boost the effects of Sinemet.

Catechol-o-methyl transferase (COMT) inhibitors are the other class of drugs frequently prescribed to enhance the effects of Sinemet. These drugs include tolcapone, marketed as Tasmar, and entacapone, marketed as Comtan. COMT inhibitors are a new type of medication that prolongs the action of Sinemet by blocking the enzyme COMT. COMT normally breaks down levodopa before it reaches the brain, so blocking this enzyme makes more levodopa available. COMT inhibitors seem to be especially helpful for patients with "on" and "off" motor fluctuations.

Because of the risk of liver damage from tolcapone, the U.S. Food and Drug Administration (FDA) has issued warnings that tolcapone should be used only in cases of advanced Parkinson's disease where nothing else helps. Patients who use tolcapone must have blood tests every two weeks to check for liver damage. Since entacapone, another COMT inhibitor, does not produce liver toxicity, doctors generally prescribe it for patients who need this type of drug.

A new medication combines entacapone with levodopa and carbidopa, all in one pill. Known as Stalevo, this drug extends the time the levodopa works, just like taking Sinemet and entacapone separately. The new combination means taking fewer pills—a convenient development for patients who need this combination.

When Surgery Is Necessary

Even with all of the modern medicines used to treat Parkinson's disease, sometimes drug treatments do not work, or their effectiveness decreases over time. Sometimes patients' symptoms in cases like this become so bad that they require surgery.

Surgical treatments for Parkinson's were first used in the 1930s, before the discovery of levodopa. Doctors did surgery to decrease tremors and other symptoms by making lesions at various points in the brain. Unfortunately, this often resulted in new problems such as paralysis.

By the 1960s doctors knew more about which areas of the brain should be targeted to control symptoms with minimal side effects. They focused on surgery in two areas—the globus pallidus and the thalamus. Destroying part of these areas seemed to reduce some of the tremors and rigidity that affected patients.

When levodopa was discovered and worked so well for many patients, these types of surgery became unpopular. But once many doctors realized that patients' symptoms frequently worsened enough to no longer be helped by medication, they began doing the surgeries again. Nowadays, with magnetic resonance imaging (MRI) of the brain available to help pinpoint the site to be operated on, surgery has become much more precise with minimal side effects, though any surgery still carries certain risks.

Today the two major surgical procedures being done are pallidotomy and deep brain stimulation. With pallidotomy, the surgeon identifies the brain site in the globus pallidus using computerized imaging, electrical recordings from the brain, and anatomic atlases. The surgeon makes a hole in the skull and passes an electrode into

A surgeon inserts an electrode into the brain of a Parkinson's patient to destroy the tissue responsible for his tremors. The patient remains conscious throughout the five-hour procedure.

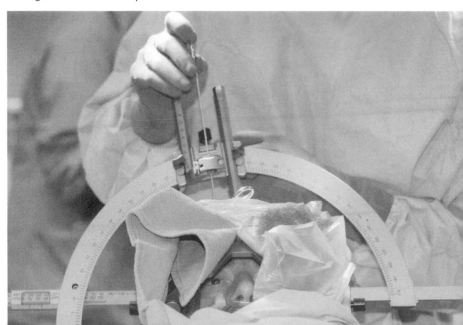

the target region. The surgeon asks the patient, who is awake, to perform certain motions to be sure the electrode is in the right place. Once the location is confirmed, the surgeon heats up the tip of the electrode and uses it to injure a small area of brain tissue. After the operation, most patients experience improvements in tremor, rigidity, bradykinesia, gait, and balance. As with any brain surgery, risks include the possibility of a stroke, bleeding, partial loss of vision and speech, swallowing difficulties, infection, and confusion.

Deep brain stimulation is the second form of surgery done on Parkinson's patients. This technique uses electrical stimulation, rather than destruction of specific areas of the brain, to control symptoms. It works by activating certain neurotransmitters. The procedure involves a surgeon identifying the area of the brain to be targeted. The doctor then makes a hole in the skull and inserts an electrode. The patient is awake throughout this procedure. Then, either immediately afterward or up to a week later, the patient undergoes general anesthesia. The surgeon connects the implanted electrode to a wire under the skin that runs to a stimulating box implanted in the chest wall. Once the box is implanted, the patient can then turn the stimulation on or off as needed.

Deep brain stimulation is usually done to the thalamus and is used to treat tremor that does not respond to drug treatment. Researchers are now working on procedures for deep brain stimulation of the globus pallidus and of the subthalamic nucleus, another part of the basal ganglia important in movement, in the hope of treating other symptoms of Parkinson's with the technique. In all cases, if the procedure does not have good results, the electrodes can be turned off or the strength of the current adjusted, so deep brain stimulation is not an irreversible or all-or-nothing procedure as is pallidotomy.

Experts say that not all patients are good candidates for deep brain stimulation. Those who respond well to Parkinson's medications, have severe tremors, and are in otherwise good health do best with the operation. Those with severe memory loss, confusion, hallucinations, or depression tend not to do well.

As with any brain surgery, deep brain stimulation carries risks of bleeding, stroke, loss of vision and speech, paralysis, and infection. The wires and chest stimulator can also cause infection or break down.

Medications to Treat Other Problems

Even with drug treatments or surgery to treat the primary symptoms of Parkinson's, many patients also require separate treatment for other problems that frequently go along with the disease. Anxiety, for example, is common and can be treated with antianxiety medications. Sleep disturbances can often be treated by adjusting Parkinson's medications or by increasing exercise and avoiding caffeine. Sometimes sleeping medications are needed, but these are not usually prescribed for Parkinson's patients because they can interact adversely with anti-Parkinson's drugs.

Depression, a very common problem in people with Parkinson's disease, also frequently warrants treatment with antidepressant drugs and/or psychotherapy. Different drugs and different types of psychotherapy work best for different patients. Treatment of depression is usually managed by a mental health specialist who consults with the physician who is treating the person for Parkinson's. According to the National Institute of Mental Health,

> Treatment for depression in the context of Parkinson's disease should be managed by a mental health professional—for example, a psychiatrist, psychologist, or clinical social worker—who is in close communication with the physician providing the Parkinson's disease treatment. This is especially important when antidepressant medication is needed or prescribed, so that potentially harmful drug interactions can be avoided. In some cases, a mental health professional that specializes in treating individuals with depression and co-occurring physical illnesses such as Parkinson's disease may be available.[14]

Other Therapies

Besides the need for psychiatric intervention, many Parkinson's patients need several other forms of therapy as part of their treatment plan. Many benefit from physical and occupational therapy. A physical therapist puts the patient through various exercises to

A Parkinson's patient works on improving her dexterity and balance during a session with a physical therapist.

increase the range of motion, dexterity, and balance. An occupational therapist teaches the patient how to adapt to movement problems and difficulties in performing daily activities. These therapists teach methods of reducing the effects of tremors and compensating for weaknesses in performing self-care and other activities. The patient learns to adapt his or her handwriting so it is more legible. Various equipment such as Velcro tabs instead of buttons on clothing and easy-to-grasp utensils are introduced. The therapist may also make recommendations for rearranging the home to make it safer and easier for the patient to navigate.

Many patients also need speech therapy to help make their speech louder and more understandable to others. There is some question as to whether traditional speech therapy is really helpful in this regard, but a new system of therapy designed specifically for Parkinson's patients shows promise. It is called the Lee Silverman Voice Method. This technique concentrates on helping the person increase speech volume by exercising the muscles of the voice box. It involves sixteen training sessions over one month, and research shows the improvements last for up to two years after treatment.

Besides the formal physical, occupational, and speech therapy that some patients receive, doctors also recommend that all Parkinson's patients get regular exercise to maintain as much mobility and flexibility as possible. Exercise also helps prevent some of the secondary symptoms such as depression from becoming major problems. Says the Parkinson's Disease Foundation, "Exercise is as important as medication for the management of PD [Parkinson's disease]."[15]

Although exercise does not stop the progression of Parkinson's disease, many people find it makes them less disabled by improving body strength and balance. The form of exercise performed does not seem to matter. Walking, swimming, aerobics, stretching, and exercises using fitness machines all seem to help.

Alternative Therapies

Since Parkinson's disease can be extremely disabling even with medication, physical and occupational therapy, and exercise, many patients are tempted to try alternative therapies advertised as being helpful or even miraculous. Experts advise people to stay away from practitioners who claim miraculous results, but say that some forms of alternative therapy can be helpful when used together with conventional anti-Parkinson's medicines and other treatments. They stress that these alternative therapies should not replace conventional treatment and that the credentials of practitioners should be carefully investigated.

Massage therapy, tai chi, and acupuncture are all alternative therapies that doctors say are not harmful and that many Parkinson's patients find helpful. Massage therapy, when provided by an accredited massage therapist, can give relief from the rigidity that patients experience. Tai chi is an ancient Chinese martial art that includes slow, flowing movements. It can significantly aid flexibility, balance, and relaxation and therefore helps reduce general disability and falling. Acupuncture is an ancient Chinese form of healing that uses fine needles inserted at various points on the skin to balance the body's energy. Many patients say that it helps alleviate pain and stiffness and makes them feel more relaxed.

Tai chi, an ancient Chinese martial art, may be beneficial to Parkinson's patients when practiced in conjunction with standard medical treatment.

Some health spas advertise that water therapies such as soaking in mineral water are helpful for people with Parkinson's disease, but doctors say these are generally not helpful. They may make people feel more relaxed and thus are not harmful, but are probably not of great benefit.

There is one alternative therapy that some Parkinson's patients try that doctors who treat the disease say should be avoided, as it can be dangerous. This is chelation therapy. Here, a practitioner gives chemicals called chelating agents intravenously. These agents supposedly remove various metals and poisons from the body. There is no evidence that chelation therapy helps patients with Parkinson's disease in any way, and it can be toxic, yet some people continue to try it in the hope of a miracle. This type of scheme is often a problem with devastating diseases like Parkinson's for which there is no cure and for which conventional treatments provide less-than-perfect results. Patients become vulnerable to unrealistic promises and sometimes suffer harm from unproven therapies that promise to help them.

Chapter 4

Living with Parkinson's Disease

E ven with proper treatment, Parkinson's disease affects nearly every aspect of a person's daily life. This can be emotionally as well as physically challenging and isolating. Says the National Institute of Neurological Disorders and Stroke:

> One of the most demoralizing aspects of the disease is how completely the patient's world changes. The most basic daily routines may be affected—from socializing with friends and enjoying normal and congenial relationships with family members to earning a living and taking care of a home. Faced with a very difficult life, people need encouragement to remain as active and involved as possible. That's when support groups can be of particular value to parkinsonian patients, their families, and their caregivers.[16]

Many patients, families, and caregivers become involved in local or national support groups and find that sharing personal stories and challenges with others going through similar situations can greatly ease the burden. "[Support groups] provide a caring environment for asking questions about Parkinson's, for laughing and crying and sharing stories and getting advice from other sufferers and for forging friendships with people who understand each other's problems,"[17] says the Parkinson's Disease Foundation. Experts say that caregivers in particular need support and respite from their duties caring for a Parkinson's patient and find that support groups can help them find local resources to ensure that their own needs and quality of life do not deteriorate to the point where they can no longer cope. This is a common problem among caregivers faced with tending to the needs of a patient with a progressive disease like Parkinson's. They often lose sight of their own needs and become increasingly frustrated by the never-ending challenge of caring for a person with extensive physical and mental disabilities.

From the Moment of Diagnosis

From the moment Parkinson's disease is diagnosed, the challenges and frustrations involved in living with it become apparent to patients and families. Dennis, a patient with Parkinson's, states, "As for many others, that moment of diagnosis was for me one of those when the world shifts on its axis, and nothing will ever again be quite what it was or where it was before." [18]

Typically, patients report feeling overwhelmed by a diagnosis of Parkinson's. Emotional numbness, sadness, disbelief, resentment, and worry are frequent responses. Some people are relieved by the diagnosis, especially when they have been through many tests in an effort to find an explanation for their symptoms. Others initially deny the reality of the diagnosis. As the National Parkinson Foundation points out, this can help some people cope and live with the early stages of the disease, as long as it does not lead the individual to refuse necessary medical treatment:

> Surprisingly, this [denial] can be a relatively healthy coping mechanism if the ability to ignore minor symptoms provides sufficient energy for the patient to carry out his or her daily routine. Most people in the early years with PD do not require assistance with self-care activities or routine chores. An occasional assist with buttons or getting an arm into the coat sleeve may suffice. If denial escalates to the point of refusing necessary medication or taking unwise risks to over-compensate for physical disabilities, it then becomes a maladaptive or unhealthy response. [19]

Spouses or other caregivers and family members also go through the emotional trauma of adjusting to the diagnosis. Some, like some patients, deny the diagnosis. Others become overprotective of the patient. Still others have difficulty dealing with the realization that they will have to provide ongoing care for a patient who is likely to become increasingly disabled.

Experts say it is often more difficult for men to accept the challenges and responsibilities of having to care for a partner with Parkinson's than it is for a woman, probably because many

When first diagnosed with Parkinson's disease, many patients, like this elderly woman, experience severe emotional trauma.

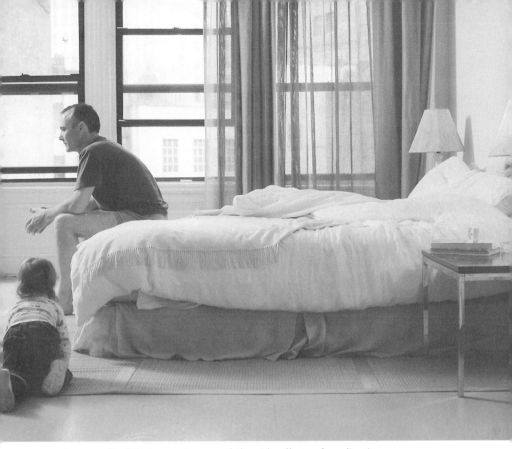

As a result of their symptoms and the side effects of medication, many Parkinson's patients with children find themselves unable to provide proper parental care.

women are more accustomed to caring for children and other family members. Others in the family such as adult children of patients with Parkinson's also seem to have difficulty adjusting to the prospect of helping with an increasingly disabled family member. As the disease progresses, decisions such as placing the patient in an assisted-living facility can add to the emotional and financial stresses for all involved.

Young children and teens with parents who are diagnosed with Parkinson's disease also face special coping challenges. Early on in the disease a parent with Parkinson's generally will still be able to care for young children adequately. As the disease progresses, however, fatigue and other symptoms, as well as side effects from medication, may render the parent unable to care for children. The spouse, relatives, and babysitters may then have to fulfill these needs, and this can be disruptive for a child.

Having a parent with a disability like Parkinson's can also affect the outlook of a child or teen either positively or negatively. As the Parkinson's Disease Foundation observes:

Having a parent with physical limitations can change a child's outlook on life for the better—especially if he or she has a positive attitude. It can allow the child the opportunity to develop compassion for those with physical challenges and feel comfortable talking to, playing with or otherwise interacting with people who are "different". On the other hand, if either parent is embarrassed by the PWP's (Person With Parkinson's) limitations or by the physical appearance of the symptoms, the child may develop the wrong outlook about physical disability. If one or both parents is always complaining about the limitations PD has caused instead of living their lives to the fullest, the child can grow up to be resentful and inconsiderate. [20]

People who live with Parkinson's and experts on the disease say that being open and honest about the condition is the key to helping children accept and understand what is happening. The level of detail revealed, of course, depends on the age of the child. But, says the Parkinson's Disease Foundation, "The key is giving your children the opportunity to express their fears, concerns, worry, or even anger so that you as their parent can offer counseling or alternative ways of coping with whatever the situation may be." [21]

Attitude and Parkinson's

Whether or not they are dealing with helping children cope with the impact of the disease, people with Parkinson's find that their own attitude often helps determine how successfully they adjust to living with the disorder, especially as symptoms worsen and the level of disability progresses. Some patients are able to maintain a positive attitude that helps them get through the bad days, whereas others become overwhelmed with negative feelings that turn their lives into an increasingly despondent burden. Phil, a patient with Parkinson's, for example, describes how he manages to remain positive and optimistic despite the disruptions that Parkinson's disease has inflicted on his life:

It is possible to maintain a positive attitude. Since the time when I was diagnosed, I have had to stop working before I wanted to, and I can no longer play the piano—something I had planned to enjoy when I retired. My medicines don't work as well as they did at the beginning, and side effects can be as bad as the disease. But a number of good things have happened which would not have occurred otherwise, and for that I am grateful. Foremost among them is that I have met some truly wonderful people. My life is different, but it is no less rich.[22]

Hilary, on the other hand, reveals how she has allowed frustration about her Parkinson's disease to impose a negative attitude about life into her existence:

For myself, I am tired of having Parkinson's. I am tired of the continual encroachment on my life, on my usefulness, and on

Muhammad Ali and Michael J. Fox, both Parkinson's patients, share a lighthearted moment. A positive outlook can help patients to cope with the disease.

the time that is available to me to be a real person. I am wasting my day on longer and longer periods of dyskinesia alternating with bradykinesia. . . . I am requiring more and more help from others to keep up the appearance of normal living, thus "wasting" their life too, time they could be giving to a more deserving cause than helping me wash a few dishes, or just get dressed.[23]

Sometimes negative feelings and frustrations about the disease contribute to the depression, anxiety, and apathy that often go along with the brain chemistry changes that underlie Parkinson's disease. Such conditions can in turn worsen the general disability and social withdrawal that many patients experience. Many people with Parkinson's no longer try to engage in activities they once enjoyed because they feel depressed, anxious, or fatigued. Many tend to avoid being with other people because they are embarrassed about their symptoms and do not want to go out where they may be seen. Although tremors, for example, are not responsible for as much disability as are many other Parkinson's symptoms, many patients are sensitive about others seeing their limbs shake and therefore avoid social situations.

The soft, slow speech and masklike facial expression frequently seen in Parkinson's disease are also common factors that contribute to social withdrawal and embarrassment. These symptoms may lead others to assume that the person with Parkinson's is unfriendly or uninterested. One patient got around this problem by telling people, "I look this way because of my Parkinson's disease. I'm actually quite friendly and interested in what you're saying."[24]

Lifestyle Adjustments Due to Impaired Mental Function

Besides the emotional and social difficulties encountered by people with Parkinson's, basic lifestyle adjustments must be made to deal with increasing disability in mental and physical functioning. Many patients experience problems with memory and slowed thinking that become severe enough to classify as dementia. This typically takes the form of forgetfulness, slowed processing of ideas,

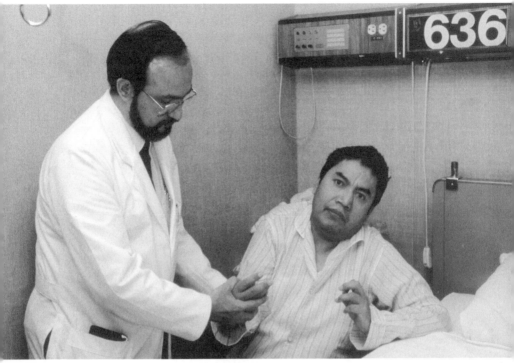

A doctor examines a Parkinson's patient. The disease may lead to impaired mental function in addition to physical disability.

difficulty concentrating, passiveness, and delays in answering questions or following through with a task.

Dementia can be due to Parkinson's disease itself or to side effects of medication. Doctors say it is important for a physician to discontinue any medication that is contributing to dementia. They also say that people who take care of a Parkinson's patient with dementia can make some changes to allow the person to participate in normal activities as much as possible. One thing that seems to help is speaking slowly and simply to the patient and allowing the person time to respond without interruption. Asking questions that require simple yes or no answers is also recommended.

Experts also advise keeping life simple by removing clutter and unneeded items from the home environment. Putting away potentially dangerous items such as knives and electrical appliances that the patient should not use is also a good idea.

Following a consistent, simple schedule and providing cues such as placing pictures of objects on drawers and pictures of what a room is for on the door are other ways of simplifying life for a patient with dementia. Pasting a list or a large calendar of to-do items for daily care and activities can also help. Alden, a Parkinson's patient with dementia, for example, helped his caregiver type a schedule to remind him of how to do things. It included reminders such as being sure to use his cane to walk to the bathroom, to take the first daily dose of medication at 7 A.M. with one-half glass of water, then brush teeth, shave, shower, and so on.

A caregiver helps a dementia patient into her car. Parkinson's patients who have developed dementia can benefit from a simple daily routine and participation in normal activities.

Experts say that people with dementia also benefit from daily mental stimulation and physical exercise. Doing word puzzles, reading, pursuing a hobby, or keeping a diary are all mentally stimulating activities that can help. Even exercise as simple as taking a walk around the block is encouraged.

Since many patients with dementia at times engage in confused or inappropriate behaviors, experts suggest that caregivers and other family members ignore such inappropriate behavior unless it is dangerous and reward desired behavior with a touch, a kiss, a smile, or a "thank you." This requires a great deal of patience and is just one of many reasons why caring for a patient with impaired mental faculties can be so challenging and frustrating.

Lifestyle Adjustments That Go Along with Increasing Physical Disability

Along with cognitive disabilities, many patients with Parkinson's encounter increasing motor disabilities that affect their daily lives. Things as simple as brushing one's teeth and getting dressed can become difficult, if not impossible. Occupational therapy can help with such difficulties, but sometimes the patient's caregiver must assist with these activities anyway. This can be tiring and frustrating for all involved.

Increasing motor difficulties also mean that many patients fall down more easily and frequently. This can be dangerous and result in broken bones and other serious injuries. Experts at the National Parkinson Foundation offer suggestions for patients to help them get around as safely as possible. These include avoiding standing with the feet too close together so as not to fall, consciously lifting the feet to avoid shuffling and subsequent falls, using a cane or walker, not carrying objects in both hands while walking since this can affect balance, consciously swinging the arms while walking to maintain balance, and not wearing rubber or crepe-soled shoes to avoid tripping.

Patients must also learn to cope with freezing spells that occur when the muscles tighten up, making the person temporarily unable to move. Sometimes this happens during "off" time when medications are wearing off, but other times it occurs unpredictably.

One woman, for instance, was shopping when she suddenly froze and was unable to move, whereas seconds earlier she had been walking comfortably. Many times doctors prescribe new combinations or long-acting anti-Parkinson's medications to avoid such incidents, but even then these freezing spells happen to some patients. In such instances, sometimes straightening the spine to generate more power to the hips and thighs, trying to step over an imaginary line on the floor, and taking several slow, deep breaths is enough to break up a freezing spell. For some patients, though, these tricks do not work, and they must receive assistance until they are able to move again on their own.

Difficulties with Eating and Swallowing

Deteriorating motor skills often also involve increasing problems with eating and swallowing that complicate everyday life and require patients to make adjustments to their accustomed lifestyle. Although most people with Parkinson's do not have to follow a special diet, some must augment a regular diet with liquid food supplements if they are losing weight or not taking in adequate nutrition. Doctors also often recommend that patients eat small meals frequently rather than three large meals per day. This is because the stomach and intestines of people with Parkinson's tend to empty more slowly than normal, and food is easier to process in smaller quantities. Eating smaller, more frequent meals also helps maintain a healthy weight.

Experts also suggest that Parkinson's patients should change their diet to include plenty of fiber and water to alleviate the constipation that often accompanies the disease. Doctors also recommend a vitamin D and calcium supplement to keep the bones strong and more resistant to fractures. Some patients must also follow a so-called protein-redistribution diet in which they consume protein only late in the day to prevent it from blocking the effects of levodopa during most of their waking hours.

Whichever diet they follow, swallowing problems can make eating a nightmare for some patients. Different people have different degrees of difficulty with various types of foods, so it is often necessary for an expert to evaluate exactly which foods are easiest for a particular patient to swallow. The person can then learn to alternate foods that are easy to swallow with those that are more difficult in order to clear out whatever accumulates in the throat and esophagus. A therapist can also introduce special exercises to make swallowing easier.

People with Parkinson's may experience difficulty swallowing, and should eat foods that can easily pass through the throat and esophagus.

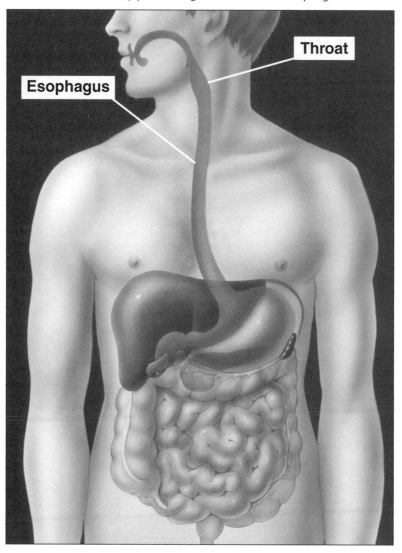

Because the muscles of the mouth and throat may not work properly in people with Parkinson's, patients may have difficulties not only in swallowing food but also with saliva. This can result in drooling. When the person is upright, drooling is not dangerous, but is embarrassing, and can contribute to a patient's avoidance of social situations. When the individual is lying down, however, the accumulation of saliva can lead to choking, so sometimes lifestyle adjustments in sleeping must be made. Some patients have to sleep in a sitting position with the head uptight. Most medications to control Parkinson's disease have no effect on drooling, and those that would control this symptom have severe adverse side effects. Consequently, most patients cannot take them and have to live with the problem from day to day.

Sleep Disturbances

Sleep disturbances that affect the quality of life are another common aspect of living with Parkinson's disease. Many times these result from anti-Parkinson's medications wearing off during the night, leading to tremors and discomfort. Sometimes sleep disturbances result from medications that cause daytime sleepiness. The person then naps during the day and is unable to sleep well at night. The dosage of medication may have to be changed if this is a problem, or the doctor may prescribe other drugs to increase alertness during the day.

Another cause of sleep disturbances may be rapid eye movement (REM) sleep disorder. REM sleep is the stage of sleep in which dreaming occurs. The eyes move rapidly back and forth during this stage. Normally, muscles in the body are relaxed during REM sleep. However, with about 25 percent of Parkinson's patients, the muscles do not relax during dream sleep. The person may then act out the dreams, sometimes hitting, kicking, or flailing around. This can be dangerous for the patient as well as for any bed partner. It also often results in the person waking up and therefore not getting enough sleep.

Experts recommend that the patient report any sleep disturbances to the physician, who can adjust medications or provide

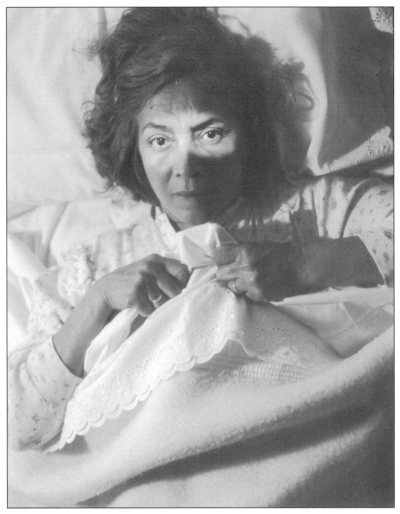

A woman with insomnia lies awake in her bed. Because Parkinson's medication can disrupt normal sleep patterns, patients commonly experience sleepless nights.

new medicines. Once the sleep disturbances lessen, the quality of waking life tends to improve.

Sensory Problems

Even if Parkinson's patients are well-rested, though, the progressive symptoms that affect them can still continue to worsen and disrupt major aspects of their lives. In addition to the mental and motor difficulties experienced, the disease can also affect the senses. Vision in particular may suffer. Many patients have trouble reading and seeing things that do not have sharp contrast such as a white rug on a white tile floor. One man was unable to see the white grab bar in his shower because it blended in with the white tile behind it. The grab bar had to be replaced with one in a contrasting color.

These visual problems tend to worsen as the disease advances. Many patients become unable even to watch television if the vision loss is serious enough. Many can no longer drive a car because of these vision problems and because of certain medications that make them sleepy. According to the Parkinson's Disease Foundation, "Problems with driving that are caused by the symptoms of PD and the effects of medications increase as the disease advances. Motor symptoms, visual and perceptual problems, and the side effects of medications (such as the 'sleep attacks' attributed to some dopamine agonists) can make the driving experience dangerous."[25]

Driving in such cases becomes a danger to the patient, to any passengers in the car, and to the general public, so sooner or later many people with the disease must give up their driving privileges. A recent National Transportation Safety Board hearing concluded that Parkinson's disease itself is not a safety hazard, but that individuals with the disease must monitor their condition so as not to drive if symptoms or side effects from medication become troublesome.

Levodopa tends to help with the visual problems associated with Parkinson's, probably because the visual system uses dopamine and is hurt by the deficiency of this neurotransmitter. But even with levodopa, many patients must make lifestyle changes in addition to not driving to cope with the loss of vision. These changes may include increasing lighting in all areas of the home and ensuring good contrast between areas such as stairs and walkways and their surroundings.

Employment and Parkinson's

Along with changes in the home and in lifestyle, many patients with advancing Parkinson's are also faced with decisions on whether they

Former president George Bush signs the Americans with Disabilities Act in 1990. The law, which prohibits discrimination against people with disabilities, has proven difficult to enforce.

can continue to work. With modern medications, most people can work for at least a while after their diagnosis, as long as these medicines successfully manage the symptoms. Those who become unable to continue to perform a job can sometimes switch jobs to a position in which symptoms of Parkinson's will not interfere.

Sometimes, though, employers will attempt to fire or demote people just because they are diagnosed with a disease like Parkinson's. The federal Americans with Disabilities Act (ADA) signed into law in 1990 prohibits any such discrimination or punishment because of a disability, but proving that this has taken place can be difficult, expensive, and time-consuming. Consequently, many employers continue to discriminate routinely against people with Parkinson's, even when the individual is still able to work effectively.

Patients who become unable to work or are fired can experience severe financial problems. Some people qualify for Social Security Disability Insurance or Supplemental Security Income, and this can help pay for living and medical expenses. However, such programs do not provide adequate funds for many people, and often it is difficult to qualify for them, so many Parkinson's sufferers continue to have financial difficulties even with help. One patient who received $736 a month in disability payments had to pay $620 per month for her medications. This left practically nothing to live on. Such problems are common among people who become disabled from Parkinson's disease.

In addition, many people who become disabled not only have to give up their jobs, but also must pay to have someone take care of them if family members cannot. Some patients become so disabled that they can no longer remain in their homes and must go to a nursing home, which is especially expensive.

Legal Issues

In addition to all the other changes in their lives that Parkinson's forces patients to face, legal experts say that it is important for anyone with such a chronic disease to ensure all personal and financial records are in order so family members can take over their management if the patient's mental or physical condition deteriorates. This includes having a will, a living will, a power of attorney, and directions for how medical care is to proceed in the event of a catastrophic medical emergency. Many people do not like to think about such issues because of unpleasant connotations associated with dying and death, but legal experts say it is important to attend to such matters sooner rather than later. Although Parkinson's disease itself does not usually directly cause death, it is responsible for progressive disability. It is therefore prudent to make arrangements for any circumstance.

Chapter 5

The Future

A GREAT DEAL of research is currently being conducted to make the lives of Parkinson's patients easier and ultimately to find a cure for the disease. The research focuses on the causes, diagnosis, and treatment of the disease. The ultimate goal of a cure—that is, a method of replacing the faulty dopamine cells in the brain—grows closer as research in each of these areas progresses.

Until recently, a problem with research into Parkinson's disease was a lack of funding. Over the past few years, however, awareness of the disease and activism to promote government and private funding have increased, partly due to the efforts of several high-profile individuals with Parkinson's.

In 1996, boxing legend Muhammad Ali, who has Parkinson's disease, lit the Olympic torch and accepted a medal from the president of the International Olympic Committee. This helped increase awareness of the disease. Ali and his wife have since been active in raising research funds and in bolstering worldwide knowledge about the disorder.

In 1998, actor Michael J. Fox disclosed that he had the illness and later set up a foundation to fund research. His efforts have contributed to a great deal more awareness and funding for Parkinson's.

Today, funding for research and outreach to the community of those affected by Parkinson's has increased dramatically, thanks to the efforts of these well-known and many lesser-known individuals. There are now hundreds of ongoing studies that promise to improve life in the foreseeable future for those affected.

Research into Diagnosis

One area where researchers hope to make progress is in developing new diagnostic techniques. Presently, diagnosis depends on a doctor's clinical evaluation, and even experienced doctors misdiagnose a substantial number of cases. Scientists hope to develop biomarkers, or easily measured biological indicators, of Parkinson's to make the diagnosis and to follow the disease's progression. This would involve brain imaging studies that can objectively determine whether or not a person has Parkinson's disease.

While neuroimaging tests are currently available to diagnose Parkinson's, they are very expensive and are therefore not used very often. Scientists are looking for newer techniques that would be available to more people. One promising technique pioneered at Harvard University uses the injected radioactive imaging agent altropane. This chemical causes dopamine neurons in the brain's substantia nigra to light up when viewed with a SPECT (single photon emission computed tomography) machine. The technique costs less than half of what existing neuroimaging methods using PET scanners cost, so doctors hope that it can be perfected and used more widely.

Muhammad Ali lights the Olympic torch in 1996. Ali's participation in the Olympic torch-lighting ceremony increased public awareness of the disease.

Research into Causes

Research into the causes of Parkinson's disease is making great strides in uncovering exactly how genetic, environmental, and biochemical influences produce the disorder. Some scientists are busy identifying which genes influence the development of the disease. Already several genes that either cause the disease directly or produce a genetic predisposition toward Parkinson's have been identified. Researchers continue to look for other genes that also play a role.

Many studies are assessing the influence of various environmental factors on causing the disease. The effects of various pesticides, herbicides, and metals are being studied to determine exactly which ones and what combinations increase the risk. This could lead to measures that would protect people from these influences, either by encouraging avoidance of certain chemicals or by banning the substances outright.

Scientists are also studying the biochemical changes that cause Parkinson's disease. In recent research at Columbia University in New York, for example, researchers found that an enzyme that causes inflammation in damaged tissues may play a role in the disease. Higher levels of this enzyme, cyclooxygenase-2 (COX-2), were in the dopamine neurons of deceased Parkinson's patients than in comparable neurons in other brains. The researchers also found higher levels of the enzyme in the brains of live mice with Parkinson's. When these mice were given a medication that inhibits COX-2, the number of surviving dopamine neurons in their brains doubled.

The Columbia scientists found that COX-2 actually causes neuron cell death through a process known as oxidative stress. Doctors say that this research indicates that medications that inhibit COX-2 may be useful in slowing the progression of Parkinson's disease. This would have to be determined through controlled studies with these drugs, which are presently used for inflammatory disorders such as arthritis.

Research into Treatment

Some research into causes, such as the COX-2 studies, end up leading to research into treatments for the disease. Other investigations are strictly designed to test new treatments, and this type of research

A Parkinson's patient relies on a specially trained dog to maintain his balance. Because drug treatments lose their effectiveness over time, patients often seek alternative ways of coping with the disease.

comprises the majority of the research into the disorder. Because existing drug treatments for Parkinson's lose their effectiveness over time and often have unpleasant side effects, investigators are constantly experimenting with new drugs to help control the symptoms and even to stop progression of the disease.

New drugs are originally developed in a laboratory and tested on laboratory animals. Once a compound has been proven to be safe and effective in a laboratory setting, the drug developer may apply to the FDA or to comparable agencies in other countries to begin testing in human clinical trials. Clinical trials involve three or four phases of testing. Once these phases are satisfactorily completed, the FDA may approve the drug for marketing, and doctors can begin prescribing the drug for people not included in the clinical trials.

Many new drugs are being tested in various phases of clinical trials and research for Parkinson's disease. One such type of drug is called an adenosine antagonist. These drugs are known to enhance the action of dopamine in laboratory animals. Researchers tested the drug istradefylline, also known as KW-6002, on humans and found that it resulted in a significant decrease in "off" time and an increase in "on" time where levodopa was effective in alleviating symptoms. Researchers plan further studies to confirm this effect in more patients and to see if KW-6002 both protects neurons from destruction and relieves symptoms.

A man wears a nicotine patch to help him quit smoking. Some studies suggest that administering certain Parkinson's drugs through the skin increases their potency.

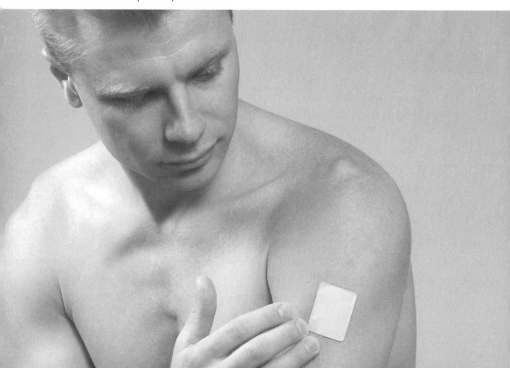

Rasagiline is another drug that seems to reduce "off" time significantly. Recent clinical trials showed that adding rasagiline to levodopa reduced "off" time by 21 percent. The drug seems to be without many adverse side effects and is administered only once a day, which is convenient for patients. Said Dr. Oliver Rascol, lead author of the rasagiline study, "I have great hope that rasagiline may help ease the burden of Parkinson's disease for a broad spectrum of patients."[26]

Another class of drugs being tested on Parkinson's patients aims to treat both cognitive and motor symptoms. While most drugs currently used affect motor symptoms, they have little effect on the cognitive decline that often accompanies the disease. One drug being tested is SIB-1508Y. In monkeys, researchers found this drug, used with low doses of levodopa, improved cognitive as well as motor symptoms. Doctors are currently in the early phases of testing this drug in humans.

Researchers are also studying new methods of delivering drugs other than orally. Rotigotine, or SPM-962, is a dopamine agonist delivered through a transdermal, or skin, patch. Studies show that a drug delivered through the skin is less likely to be broken down and therefore may allow the use of lower doses. Doctors are hopeful that clinical trials will prove this drug delivered transdermally to be effective in reducing symptoms of Parkinson's. Another area of investigation is how effective in alleviating symptoms is an implantable pump that gives a continuous supply of levodopa.

Along with more effectively relieving symptoms, several new drugs, doctors hope, may protect dopamine neurons from the damage that results in Parkinson's disease. The National Institute of Neurological Disorders and Stroke is conducting a study on previously untreated Parkinson's patients to see if the drugs minocycline and creatine protect neurons in the brain and thus prevent progression of the disease. Previous research shows these agents exhibit neuroprotective properties in the laboratory. Minocycline is an antibiotic that acts as an anti-inflammatory and prevents cells from dying. Creatine is a dietary supplement shown to increase the amount of the chemical phosphocreatine in the brain. This chemical protects neurons from injury.

A recent study at the University of California, San Diego, showed that another dietary supplement commonly sold in drugstores may also be neuroprotective and slow the early development of Parkinson's disease. The supplement is called coenzyme Q10. Doctors are not sure how it protects against progression of the disease, but say it may have to do with the fact that coenzyme Q10 plays a role in cell energy production. Patients taking 1200 milligrams per day of the supplement showed the best results, as indicated by a standard rating scale for measuring Parkinson's symptoms. However, doctors do not yet know how coenzyme Q10 interacts with Parkinson's medications such as levodopa and therefore caution patients who take such medications not to begin taking coenzyme Q10 without consulting their doctors.

Another drug that shows promise in protecting neurons is one currently used to treat epilepsy. A team of scientists led by Dr. Serge Przedborski at Columbia University found that giving mice with

In addition to drugs, other methods to treat Parkinson's are being developed. Implanted in the brain, this device disrupts the signals responsible for tremors and other symptoms of the disease.

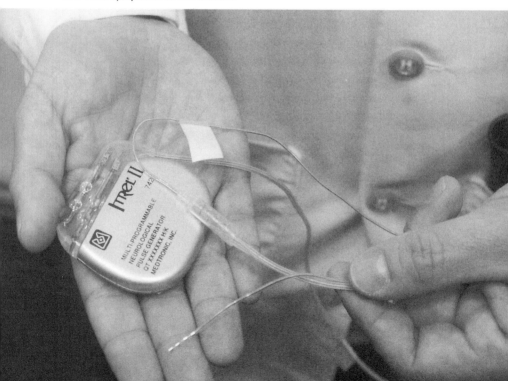

Parkinson's disease the drug D-b-hydroxybutyrate (DbHB) restored impaired brain function and protected against degeneration of the nervous system. The DbHB appeared to act by restoring the function of mitochondria in cells that produce dopamine. Mitochondria are known to play a role in the cell destruction that underlies Parkinson's. Restoring the mitochondrial function prevented the level of dopamine from decreasing, thereby diminishing symptoms of Parkinson's disease in the mice. The researchers hope that further testing will show this drug to be useful in humans as well.

The experimental drugs pifithrinapha (PFT) and Z-1-117 also show promise in restoring cell mitochondrial function to protect dopamine neurons from destruction. These drugs, used as experimental cancer treatments, also have applications against Parkinson's disease. Investigators at the National Institute on Aging found that dopamine neurons treated with these drugs were more resistant to being killed by environmental toxins and pesticides that increase the risk of Parkinson's. The researchers believe the drugs work by blocking the action of a protein known as P53. P53 promotes the death of dopamine neurons by causing an increase in the permeability of membranes surrounding the cells' mitochondria. This means that chemicals can leak out and destroy the cells. By blocking P53, this process is prevented. The investigators hope that if further testing shows these drugs to be safe in laboratory animals, someday they can be tested in humans as a treatment for Parkinson's disease.

Research on Growth Factors

A line of research related to the search for protective drugs to treat Parkinson's involves using growth factors to promote brain cell growth and therefore to reverse the progression of the disease. Researchers at the Institute of Neurosciences in Bristol, England, recently found that dripping a protein known as glial cell line–derived neurotrophic factor, or GDNF, into the brains of patients with advanced Parkinson's disease diminished their symptoms. One patient who was in constant pain and barely able to walk is now able to walk several miles each day. GDNF also reduced or stopped tremors in several people.

GDNF has been shown in previous research with laboratory animals to nourish and regenerate brain cells that die from Parkinson's disease. The regenerated brain cells then begin to produce dopamine. The researchers say that GDNF is the first treatment that seems to reverse, rather than just slow down, the progression of Parkinson's. Further testing is planned on more patients. If the treatment continues to give positive results and proves to be safe, experts say it could represent a huge step forward in Parkinson's research. Said Dr. Michael Zigmond of the University of Pittsburgh School of Medicine, a Parkinson's disease expert who was not involved in the research, "I consider this study to be the most exciting advance in the treatment of Parkinson's disease that has come about in years."[27]

Stem Cell Research

Another brand new area of promising treatment for Parkinson's disease is stem cell research. Stem cells are cells that have the potential to develop into any kind of cell in the body. Researchers hope that a method will be discovered of enabling stem cells to develop into brain cells that could replace the cells destroyed by Parkinson's disease.

Recently, scientists in Scotland and Japan made a discovery that significantly advanced the understanding of stem cells. They found an element they named Nanog that enables stem cells to retain their ability to mature into any type of cell. The name Nanog is taken from that of a mythical land in a Celtic legend, Tir nan og, where residents remained forever young.

Since these investigators now know what is necessary for stem cells to mature into any other type of cell, this discovery brings scientists closer to being able to turn ordinary cells into stem cells by using Nanog in some fashion. This is desirable because, at the present time, stem cells are generally taken from human embryos or umbilical cord cells. There is a great deal of controversy over the use of embryonic cells since their use requires destruction of the embryo.

Other recent work related to stem cells was performed by Dr. Eva Mezey and others at the National Institute of Neurological Disorders and Stroke. Mezey and her colleagues found that stem cells from bone marrow, the soft tissue inside bone cavities where blood cells form, can enter the human brain and form new neurons and

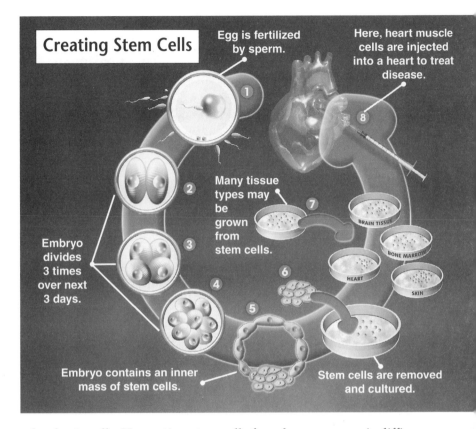

Creating Stem Cells

Egg is fertilized by sperm.

Here, heart muscle cells are injected into a heart to treat disease.

Many tissue types may be grown from stem cells.

BRAIN TISSUE

BONE MARROW

HEART

SKIN

Embryo divides 3 times over next 3 days.

Embryo contains an inner mass of stem cells.

Stem cells are removed and cultured.

other brain cells. Harvesting stem cells from bone marrow is difficult, however, so the procedure of stem cell transplants from this source is not done frequently.

The Mezey research team performed the study on brain tissue taken at autopsy from female patients who had received bone marrow transplants from male donors. Examination of the brain tissue showed glial cells and neurons containing Y chromosomes, which only appear in cells from a male. This meant that some of the transplanted stem cells migrated to the brain to form new brain cells. The researchers believe that stem cells may migrate to areas of the brain that give off signals indicating damage that requires new cells. They plan to do further studies to determine what these signals might be in the hope of developing methods of prompting stem cell migration to the brain. If this can be achieved, it could lead to new methods of treating Parkinson's and other diseases that result from a loss of certain brain cells.

Related to stem cell research is an experimental surgery called a brain tissue transplant. Here, brain tissue destined to become substantia nigra cells is taken from a human fetus, from genetically engineered cells, or from animal cells. The cells are implanted into the brain of a person with Parkinson's disease. Scientists hope that these cells will produce dopamine and thereby relieve symptoms of the disorder. Thus far, there is not enough data to be sure that this method will work.

Gene Therapy

Another new avenue of research into treating Parkinson's disease is gene therapy. In 2003 doctors at New York Presbyterian Hospital performed the first gene therapy operation on a Parkinson's patient. The physicians bored a hole in the person's skull and infused 3.5 billion viral particles containing copies of a human gene into the brain. Genes themselves cannot get into cells, but viruses can, so they are often used to get genes into living cells in gene therapy experiments. The viruses are altered so as not to produce infection. The genes they introduced in this study were supposed to stimulate cells in the subthalamic nucleus region of the brain to make the neurotransmitter gamma-aminobutyric acid (GABA). GABA has been shown to calm overactive nerve cells that can contribute to Parkinson's symptoms. In previous experiments with mice, the gene therapy significantly helped over half of the animals by diminishing symptoms. Whether this will happen in humans remains to be seen.

Although the doctors performing the human research have high hopes for success, some other gene therapy experts are concerned about adverse effects either from the viruses used to introduce the genes or from the genes themselves. In 1999, a teenage boy named Jesse Gelsinger died in a gene therapy experiment at the University of Pennsylvania. More recently, several children in France treated with gene therapy developed leukemia. Such past problems

A doctor examines the fingers of a Parkinson's patient to determine their range of motion. As funding for Parkinson's disease continues to increase, researchers are optimistic about the prospects for a cure.

with this technique have led many doctors to be skeptical about the value and safety of gene therapy, but research in this direction is still continuing.

Other research in June 2003 pioneered still another gene-related treatment technique that may someday prove effective against Parkinson's disease. Dr. Henry Paulson and his associates at the University of Iowa experimented with a method of shutting down mutant gene expression in the brain. The method is called RNA interference. The investigators used it to turn off mutant genes in laboratory cell cultures. This method uses small fragments of genetic material known as small interfering RNA to attach to and inactivate certain abnormal gene sequences. The technique only targets mutant genes and allows normal genes to maintain their function.

The investigators in this study plan to test the RNA interference method in laboratory animals to see whether it will work in animals with specific diseases like Parkinson's. If it does, this could lead to a cure for the form of Parkinson's caused by a mutant gene. "The ultimate goal is to cure or prevent disease with a one-time injection that will forever suppress the mutation in affected patients,"[28] said one of the investigators.

Improving Existing Surgeries

Besides the research into entirely new techniques of treatment like RNA interference and gene therapy, some research on treatment is focusing on improving existing surgery for Parkinson's. The National Institute of Neurological Disorders and Stroke, for example, recently launched a clinical trial for deep brain stimulation using a more advanced stimulator than is currently used in this type of surgery. Deep brain stimulation is used to stop the uncontrollable movements that characterize Parkinson's disease. The researchers hope that this new study will give doctors a better weapon against these symptoms. They are also comparing deep brain stimulation in various sites in the brain to see which places yield the best results.

Hope for the Future

The object of all this research into treatments, causes, and diagnosis of Parkinson's disease is, of course, to make the lives of those who suffer with the disorder easier and to someday find a cure. No one knows how long it will take to achieve these goals, but according to the National Institutes of Health, the possibility of successful new treatments and even a cure looks more promising all the time. "A new optimism that Parkinson's disease can be defeated is energizing the research community and patient advocates," says a National Institutes of Health report. "Halting the progression of Parkinson's disease, restoring lost function, and even preventing the disease are all realistic goals."[29]

Notes

Introduction: An Ancient Disease

1. Quoted in Gerald M. Stern, ed., *Parkinson's Disease*. Baltimore: Johns Hopkins University Press, 1990, p. xxiii.
2. Quoted in Who Named It?, "James Parkinson," www.whonamed it.com/doctor.cfm/392.html.

Chapter 1: What Is Parkinson's Disease?

3. William J. Weiner, Lisa M. Shulman, and Anthony E. Lang, *Parkinson's Disease: A Complete Guide for Patients and Families.* Baltimore: Johns Hopkins University Press, 2001, p. 10.
4. National Institute of Neurological Disorders and Stroke, "Parkinson's Disease: Hope Through Research," www.ninds.nih.gov/health_and_medical/pubs/parkinson_disease_htr.htm.
5. Weiner, Shulman, and Lang, *Parkinson's Disease*, p. 97.
6. Steven Frucht and Robin Elliot, "How Is Parkinson's Diagnosed?" www.pdf.org/aboutPDF/diagnosing_parkinsons.cfm.
7. Quoted in Barbara Blake-Krebs and Linda Herman, *When Parkinson's Strikes Early.* Alameda, CA: Hunter, 2001, p. 11.

Chapter 2: What Causes Parkinson's Disease?

8. Parkinson's Disease Foundation, "Nine Scientific Pathways to Understanding Parkinson's," www.pdf.org/aboutPDF/nine_pathways.cfm.
9. Quoted in Dukemed News, "Gene Linked to Late-Onset Parkinson's Disease," http://dukemednews.duke.edu/news/article.php?id=5091.
10. Quoted in National Institute of Environmental Health Sciences, "Combination of Two Widely Used Pesticides Linked

to Parkinson's Disease," www.niehs.nih.gov/centers/2001news/
ctrnews5.htm.

Chapter 3: How Is Parkinson's Disease Treated?

11. National Parkinson Foundation, "Summary Points Regarding Dopaminergic Therapy," www.parkinson.org/med20.htm.
12. Weiner, Shulman, and Lang, *Parkinson's Disease*, p. 146.
13. Weiner, Shulman, and Lang, *Parkinson's Disease*, p. 156.
14. National Institute of Mental Health, "Depression and Parkinson's Disease," www.nimh.nih.gov/publicat/depparkinson.cfm.
15. Parkinson's Disease Foundation, "The Role of the Patient," www.pdf.org/AboutPD/roleofpatient.cfm.

Chapter 4: Living with Parkinson's Disease

16. National Institute of Neurological Disorders and Stroke, "Parkinson's Disease: Hope Through Research."
17. Parkinson's Disease Foundation, "The Role of the Patient."
18. Quoted in Blake-Krebs and Herman, *When Parkinson's Strikes Early*, p. 26.
19. Susan Imke, Trudy Hutton, and Sheree Loftus, "Caring and Coping," National Parkinson Foundation, www.parkinson.org/caring.htm.
20. Parkinson's Disease Foundation, "Parenthood and Parkinson's Disease," www.pdf.org/aboutPDF/parenthood.cfm.
21. Parkinson's Disease Foundation, "Parenthood and Parkinson's Disease."
22. Quoted Blake-Krebs and Herman, *When Parkinson's Strikes Early*, p. 28.
23. Quoted in Blake-Krebs and Herman, *When Parkinson's Strikes Early*, p. 40.
24. Quoted in Weiner, Shulman, and Lang, *Parkinson's Disease*, p. 47.
25. Parkinson's Disease Foundation, "Driving with Parkinson's: A Public Safety Hazard?" www.pdf.org/aboutPDF/driving_with_parkinsons.cfm.

Chapter 5: The Future

26. Quoted in Parkinson's Disease Foundation, "Research Shows Rasagiline Reduces 'Off' Time," www.pdf.org/News/news.cfm?

selectedItem=117&type=1&returnURL=news%2Ecfm%3Ftype%
3D1.

27. Quoted in Parkinson's Disease Foundation, "Brain-Cell Growth
Protein Shows Promise for Parkinson's Patients in Early Human
Trial," www.pdf.org/News/news.cfm?selectedItem=105&type=
1&returnURL=news%2Ecfm%3Ftype%3D1.

28. Quoted in National Institute of Neurological Disorders and Stroke,
"Investigators Explore Selective Silencing of Disease Genes,"
www.ninds.nih.gov/news_and_events/news_article_gene_
silencing.htm.

29. Quoted in Blake-Krebs and Herman, *When Parkinson's Strikes
Early*, p. 154.

Glossary

alpha-synuclein: Protein that aids in nerve cell communication and that clumps abnormally in Parkinson's disease.

apoptosis: A form of cell death scientists believe is involved in the development of Parkinson's disease.

basal ganglia: The large gray mass at the base of the brain that coordinates movement.

bradykinesia: Slowness of movement that is one of the primary symptoms of Parkinson's disease.

chromosome: Wormlike body in the center of a cell that houses genetic information.

dopamine: The primary neurotransmitter that is deficient in Parkinson's disease.

dyskinesia: Involuntary writhing movements that are often side effects of anti-Parkinson's medications.

free radical: Unstable molecule that contributes to nerve cell death.

gene: The part of a DNA molecule that passes hereditary information from parents to their offspring.

globus pallidus: An area of the brain that often shows abnormal cell activity; associated with certain symptoms of Parkinson's disease.

Lewy bodies: Abnormal clumps of alpha-synuclein proteins in nerve cells thought to play a role in the development of Parkinson's disease.

mitochondria: Small energy-producing bodies within cells.

mutation: Damage to a gene or chromosome that can cause certain diseases or disorders.

neurologist: A doctor who specializes in disorders of the nervous system.

neuron: A nerve cell.

neurotransmitter: A brain chemical messenger.

pallidotomy: Surgery that uses an electrode to destroy cells in the globus pallidus to treat some symptoms of Parkinson's disease.

parkinsonism: A neurological disorder that shares some symptoms of Parkinson's disease but results from different processes.

Parkinson's disease: A chronic, progressive disease of the nervous system characterized by tremor, rigidity, slow movement, and balance problems.

striatum: Part of the basal ganglia that is affected by Parkinson's disease.

substantia nigra: An area of the brain that is damaged in Parkinson's disease. The term means black substance because the cells in the area are dark.

Organizations to Contact

American Parkinson Disease Association
1250 Hylan Blvd.
Suite 4B
Staten Island, NY 10305
(800) 223-2732 or
(718) 981-8001
www.apdaparkinson.org

Provides information on research, patient services, education, and raising public awareness of the disease.

Michael J. Fox Foundation for Parkinson's Research
Grand Central Station
PO Box 4777
New York, NY 10163
(800) 708-7644 or
(212) 509-0995
www.michaeljfox.org

Organization dedicated to finding a cure for Parkinson's disease by sponsoring research.

National Institute of Neurological Disorders and Stroke (NINDS)
NIH Neurological Institute
PO Box 5801
Bethesda, MD 20824
(800) 352-9924 or
(301) 496-5751
www.ninds.nih.gov

Government agency providing information and research about all aspects of Parkinson's disease.

National Parkinson Foundation
Bob Hope Parkinson Research Center
1501 NW 9th Ave.
Miami, FL 33136-1494
(800) 327-4545 or
(305) 243-6666
www.parkinson.org
Provides information on research, education, referrals, and care.

Parkinson's Disease Foundation
710 W. 168th St.
New York, NY 10032-9982
(800) 457-6676 or
(212) 923-4700
www.pdf.org
Provides comprehensive education, advocacy, and research funding on all aspects of Parkinson's disease.

For Further Reading

Elaine Landau, *Parkinson's Disease.* London: Franklin Watts, 1999.
   Discusses symptoms, diagnosis, treatment, and coping strategies.
Alvin Silverstein, Virginia B. Silverstein, and Laura Silverstein Nunn,
   Parkinson's Disease. Berkeley Heights, NJ: Enslow, 2002. Discusses
   history, causes, diagnosis, treatment, and real-life stories.

Works Consulted

Books

Barbara Blake-Krebs and Linda Herman, *When Parkinson's Strikes Early*. Alameda, CA: Hunter 2001. Personal stories of young-onset Parkinson's patients.

Gerald M. Stern, ed., *Parkinson's Disease*. Baltimore: Johns Hopkins University Press, 1990. Highly technical medical book.

William J. Weiner, Lisa M. Shulman, and Anthony E. Lang, *Parkinson's Disease: A Complete Guide for Patients and Families*. Baltimore: Johns Hopkins University Press, 2001. Comprehensive guide to understanding and living with Parkinson's disease.

Periodicals

W. Bara-Jiminez et al., "Adenosine A2A Receptor Antagonist Treatment of Parkinson's Disease," *Neurology*, 2003, vol. 61.

J.H. Bower et al, "Head Trauma Preceding PD," *Neurology*, 2003, vol. 60.

Honglei Chen et al., "Weight Loss in Parkinson Disease," *Annals of Neurology*, 2003, vol. 53.

Andrew Feigin, "Non-Dopaminergic-Symptomatic Therapies for Parkinson's Disease Turn On or Turn Off?" *Neurology*, 2003, vol. 61.

Robert A. Hauser et al., "Randomized Trial of the Adenosine A2A Receptor Antagonist Istradefylline in Advanced PD," *Neurology*, vol. 61.

National Institutes of Health, "Bone Marrow Generates New Neurons in Human Brains," *NIH News*, January 20, 2003.

Jerrold L. Vitek et al., "Trial of Pallidotomy Versus Medical Therapy for Parkinson Disease," *Annals of Neurology*, 2003, vol. 53.

Internet Sources

The American Occupational Therapy Association, "Parkinson's Disease: How Occupational Therapy Can Help," www.aota.org/featured/area6/links/link02am.asp.

DukemedNews, "Gene Linked to Late-Onset Parkinson's Disease," http://dukemednews.duke.edu/news/article.php?id=5091.

Steven Frucht and Robin Elliot, "How Is Parkinson's Diagnosed?" www.pdf.org/aboutPDF/diagnosing_parkinsons.cfm.

Susan Imke, Trudy Hutton, and Sheree Loftus, "Caring and Coping," National Parkinson Foundation, www.parkinson.org/caring.htm.

National Institute of Environmental Health Sciences, "Combination of Two Widely Used Pesticides Linked to Parkinson's Disease," www.niehs.nih.gov/centers/2001news/ctrnews5.htm.

National Institute of Mental Health, "Depression and Parkinson's Disease," www.nimh.nih.gov/publicat/depparkinson.cfm.

National Institute of Neurological Disorders and Stroke, "Investigators Explore Selective Silencing of Disease Genes," www.ninds.nih.gov/news_and_events/news_article_gene_silencing.htm.

———, "Parkinson's Disease: Hope Through Research," www.ninds.nih.gov/health_and_medical/pubs/parkinson_disease_htr.htm.

National Parkinson Foundation, "A Discussion of Alternative Medicine," www.parkinson.org/med54.htm.

———, "Encouraging News About Treatment for Advanced Parkinson's Disease," www.parkinson.org/rasagilinenews.htm.

———, "Neuroprotective Agents for Clinical Trials in Parkinson's Disease," www.parkinson.org/protectagentspd.htm.

———, "Parkinson's Disease Risks Associated with Dietary Iron, Manganese, and Other Nutrient Intakes," www.parkinson.org/dietaryiron.htm.

———, "Summary Points Regarding Dopaminergic Therapy," www.parkinson.org/med20.htm.

———, "The Unified Parkinson Rating Scale," www.parkinson.org/unifiedpd_rating.htm.

Parkinson's Disease Foundation, "Brain-Cell Growth Protein Shows Promise for Parkinson's Patients in Early Human Trial," www.pdf.org/News/news.cfm?selectedItem=105&type=1&returnURL=news%2Ecfm%3Ftype%3D1.

————, "Driving with Parkinson's: A Public Safety Hazard?" www.pdf.org/aboutPDF/driving_with_parkinsons.cfm.

————, "Nine Scientific Pathways to Understanding Parkinson's," www.pdf.org/aboutPDF/nine_pathways.cfm.

————, "Parenthood and Parkinson's Disease," www.pdf.org/aboutPDF/parenthood.cfm.

————, "Research Shows Rasagiline Reduces 'Off' Time," www.pdf.org/News/news.cfm?selectedItem=117&type=1&return URL=news%2Ecfm%3Ftype%3D1.

———— "The Role of the Patient." www.pdf.org/AboutPD/roleof patient.cfm.

Juan Sanchez-Ramos, "Parkinson Disease at an Early Age," www.parkinson.org/earlypd.htm.

Who Named It?, "James Parkinson," www.whonamedit.com/doctor.cfm/392.html.

Index

Picture Credits

About the Author

Melissa Abramovitz grew up in San Diego, California, and, as a teenager, developed an interest in medical topics. She began college with the intention of becoming a doctor but later switched majors, graduating summa cum laude from the University of California, San Diego, with a degree in psychology in 1976.

Launching her career as a freelance writer in 1986 to allow herself to be an at-home mom when her two children were small, she realized she had found her niche. She continues to write regularly for a variety of magazines and educational book publishers. In her eighteen years as a freelancer she has published hundreds of nonfiction articles and numerous short stories, poems, and books for children, teens, and adults. Many of her works are on medical topics.

At present she lives in San Luis Obispo, California, with her husband, two college-age sons, and two dogs.